ARADIA
OR THE GOSPEL OF THE WITCHES

ARADIA
OR THE GOSPEL OF THE WITCHES

BY

CHARLES G. LELAND

KALPAZ

ISBN: 978-93-5128-997-5(HB)

First Published in 1899
Indian Reprint in 2017

Published by

Kalpaz Publications
C-30, Satyawati Nagar,
Delhi – 110052
E-mail: kalpaz@hotmail.com
Website: kalpazpublications.com
Ph.: +91-9212142040

PREFACE

If the reader has ever met with the works of the learned folk-lorist G. Pitré, or the articles contributed by "Lady Vere de Vere" to the Italian *Rivista*, or that of J. H. Andrews to *Folk-Lore*,[1] he will be aware that there are in Italy great numbers of *strege*, fortune-tellers or witches, who divine by cards, perform strange ceremonies in which spirits are supposed to be invoked, make and sell amulets, and, in fact, comport themselves generally as their reputed kind are wont to do, be they Black Voodoos in America or sorceresses anywhere.

But the Italian *strega* or sorceress is in certain respects a different character from these. In most cases she comes of a family in which her calling or art has been practised for many generations. I have no doubt that there are instances in which the ancestry remounts to mediæval, Roman, or it may be Etruscan times. The result has naturally been the accumulation in such families of much tradition. But in Northern

[1] March, 1897: "Neapolitan Witchcraft."

Italy, as its literature indicates, though there has been some slight gathering of fairy tales and popular superstitions by scholars, there has never existed the least interest as regarded the strange lore of the witches, nor any suspicion that it embraced an incredible quantity of old Roman minor myths and legends, such as OVID has recorded, but of which much escaped him and all other Latin writers.[1]

This ignorance was greatly aided by the wizards and witches themselves, in making a profound secret of all their traditions, urged thereto by fear of the priests. In fact, the latter all unconsciously actually contributed immensely to the preservation of such lore, since the charm of the forbidden is very great, and witchcraft, like the truffle, grows best and has its raciest flavour when most deeply hidden. However this may be, both priest and wizard are vanishing now with incredible rapidity—it has even struck a French writer that a Franciscan in a railway carriage is a strange

[1] Thus we may imagine what the case would have been as regards German fairy-tales if nothing had survived to a future day except the collections of GRIMM and MUSÆUS. The world would fall into the belief that these constituted all the works of the kind which had ever existed, when, in fact, they form only a small part of the whole. And folklore was unknown to classic authors: there is really no evidence in any ancient Latin writer that he gathered traditions and the like among the vulgar, as men collect at present. They all made books entirely out of books—there being still "a few left of the same sort" of literati.

anomaly—and a few more years of newspapers and bicycles (Heaven knows what it will be when flying-machines appear !) will probably cause an evanishment of all.

However, they die slowly, and even yet there are old people in the Romagna of the North who know the Etruscan names of the Twelve Gods, and invocations to Bacchus, Jupiter, and Venus, Mercury, and the Lares or ancestral spirits, and in the cities are women who prepare strange amulets, over which they mutter spells, all known in the old Roman time, and who can astonish even the learned by their legends of Latin gods, mingled with lore which may be found in CATO or THEOCRITUS. With one of these I became intimately acquainted in 1886, and have ever since employed her specially to collect among her sisters of the hidden spell in many places all the traditions of the olden time known to them. It is true that I have drawn from other sources, but this woman by long practice has perfectly learned what few understand, or just what I want, and how to extract it from those of her kind.

Among other strange relics, she succeeded, after many years, in obtaining the following "Gospel," which I have in her handwriting. A full account of its nature with many details will be found in an Appendix. I do not know definitely whether my informant derived a part of these traditions from *written* sources or oral narration, but believe it was chiefly the latter. However, there are a few wizards who copy or preserve documents relative to their art. I have not seen my collector since the "Gospel" was sent to me. I hope at some future time to be better informed.

For brief explanation I may say that witchcraft is known to its votaries as *la vecchia religione*, or the old religion, of which DIANA is the Goddess, her daughter *Aradia* (or Herodias) the female Messiah, and that this little work sets forth how the latter was born, came down to earth, established witches and witchcraft, and then returned to heaven. With it are given the ceremonies and invocations or incantations to be addressed to *Diana* and *Aradia*, the exorcism of Cain, and the spells of the holy-stone, rue, and verbena, constituting, as the text declares, the regular church-service, so to speak, which is to be chanted or pronounced at the witch-meetings. There are also included the very curious incantations or benedictions of the honey, meal, and salt, or cakes of the witch-supper, which is curiously classical, and evidently a relic of the Roman Mysteries.

The work could have been extended *ad infinitum* by adding to it the ceremonies and incantations which actually form a part of the Scripture of Witchcraft, but as these are nearly all—or at least in great number—to be found in my works entitled *Etruscan-Roman Remains* and *Legends of Florence*, I have hesitated to compile such a volume before ascertaining whether there is a sufficiently large number of the public who would buy such a work.

Since writing the foregoing I have met with and read a very clever and entertaining work entitled *Il Romanzo dei Settimani*, G. CAVAGNARI, 1889, in which the author, in the form of a novel, vividly depicts the manners, habits of thought, and especially the nature of witchcraft, and the many superstitions current among the peasants in Lombardy. Unfortunately, notwithstanding his extensive knowledge of the subject, it never seems to have once occurred to the narrator that these traditions were anything but noxious nonsense or abominably un-Christian folly. That there exist in them *marvellous* relics of ancient mythology and valuable folklore, which is the very *cor cordium* of history, is as uncared for by him as it would be by a common *Zoccolone* or tramping Franciscan. One would think it might have been suspected by a man who knew that a witch really endeavoured to kill seven people as a ceremony or rite, in order to get the secret of endless wealth, that such a sorceress *must* have had a store of wondrous legends; but of all this there is no trace, and it is very evident that nothing could be further from his mind than that there was anything *interesting* from a higher or more genial point of view in it all.

His book, in fine, belongs to the very great number of those written on ghosts and superstition since the latter has fallen into discredit, in which the authors indulge in much satirical and very safe but cheap ridicule of what to them is merely vulgar and false. Like Sir Charles Coldstream, they have peeped into the crater of Vesuvius after it had ceased to "erupt," and found "nothing in it." But there was something in it once; and the man of science, which Sir Charles was not, still finds a great deal in the remains, and the antiquarian a Pompeii or a Herculaneum—'tis said there are still *seven* buried cities to unearth. I have done what little (it is really very little) I could, to disinter something from the dead volcano of Italian sorcery.

If this be the manner in which Italian witchcraft is treated by the most intelligent writer who has depicted it, it will not be deemed remarkable that there are few indeed who will care whether there is a veritable Gospel of the Witches, apparently of extreme antiquity, embodying the belief in a strange counter-religion which has held its own from pre-historic time to the present day. "Witchcraft is all rubbish, or something worse," said old writers, "and therefore all books about it are nothing better." I sincerely trust, however, that these pages may fall into the hands of at least a few who will think better of them.

I should, however, in justice to those who do care to explore dark and bewildering paths, explain clearly that witch-lore is hidden with most scrupulous care from all save a very few in Italy, just as it is among the Chippeway Medas or the Black Voodoo. In the novel to the life of *I Settimani* an aspirant is represented as living with a witch and acquiring or picking up with pain, scrap by scrap, her spells and incantations, giving years to it. So my friend the late M. DRAGOMANOFF told me how a certain man in Hungary, having learned that he had collected many spells (which were indeed subsequently published in folklore journals), stole into the scholar's room and surreptitiously copied them, so that the next year when DRAGOMANOFF returned, he found the thief in full practice as a blooming magician. Truly he had not got many incantations, only a dozen or so, but a very little will go a great way in the business, and I venture to say there is perhaps hardly a single witch in Italy who knows as many as I have published, mine having been assiduously collected from many, far and wide. Everything of the kind which is written is, moreover, often destroyed with scrupulous care by priests or penitents, or the vast number who have a superstitious fear of even being in the same house with such documents, so that I regard the rescue of the *Vangelo* as something which is to say the least remarkable.

CONTENTS

ARADIA

OR THE

GOSPEL OF THE WITCHES

CHAPTER I

HOW DIANA GAVE BIRTH TO ARADIA (HERODIAS)

"It is Diana! Lo!
She rises crescented."
—KEATS' *Endymion*.

"Make more bright
The Star Queen's crescent on her marriage night."
—*Ibid.*

THIS is the Gospel (*Vangelo*) of the Witches:

DIANA greatly loved her brother LUCIFER, the god of the Sun and of the Moon, the god of Light (*Splendor*), who was so proud of his beauty, and who for his pride was driven from Paradise.

DIANA had by her brother a daughter, to whom they gave the name of ARADIA [*i.e.* Herodias].

In those days there were on earth many rich and many poor.

The rich made slaves of all the poor.

In those days were many slaves who were cruelly treated; in every palace tortures, in every castle prisoners.

Many slaves escaped. They fled to the country; thus they became thieves and evil folk. Instead of sleeping by night, they plotted escape and robbed their masters, and then slew them. So they dwelt in the mountains and forests as robbers and assassins, all to avoid slavery.

DIANA said one day to her daughter ARADIA:

E vero che tu sei uno spirito,
Ma tu sei nata per essere ancora
Mortale, e tu devi andare
Sulla terra e fare da maestra
A donne e a' uomini che avranno
Volentà di inparare la tua scuola
Che sara composta di stregonerie.

Non devi essere come la figlia di Caino,
E della razza che sono divenuti
Scellerati infami a causa dei maltrattamenti,
Come Giudei e Zingari,
Tutti ladri e briganti,
Tu non divieni. . . .

Tu sarai (sempre) la prima strega,
La prima strega divenuta nel mondo,
Tu insegnerai l' arte di avvelenare,
Di avvelenare (tutti) i signori,
Di farli morti nei loro palazzi,

Di legare il spirito del oppressore,
E dove si trova un contadino ricco e avaro,
Insegnerai alle strege tue alunne,
Come rovinare il suo raccolto
Con tempesta, folgore e balen,
Con grandine e vento.

Quando un prete ti fara del male,
Del male colle sue bene di' Zioni,
Tu le farai (sempre) un doppio male
Col mio nome, col nome di *Diana*,
Regina delle strege. . . .

Quando i nobili e i preti vi diranno
Dovete credere nel Padre, Figlio,
E Maria, rispondete gli sempre,
"Il vostro dio Padre e Maria
Sono tre diavoli. . . .

"Il vero dio Padre non e il vostro—
Il vostro dio—io sono venuta
Per distruggere la gente cattiva
E la distruggero. . . .

"Voi altri poveri soffrite anche la fame,
E lavorato malo e molte volte;
Soffrite anche la prigione;
Mapero avete una anima,
Una anima più buona, e nell' altra,
Nell' altra mondo voi starete bene,
E gli altri male." . . .

Translation.

'Tis true indeed that thou a spirit art,
But thou wert born but to become again
A mortal; thou must go to earth below
To be a teacher unto women and men
Who fain would study witchcraft in thy school

Yet like Cain's daughter thou shalt never be,
Nor like the race who have become at last
Wicked and infamous from suffering,
As are the Jews and wandering Zingari,
Who are all thieves and knaves; like unto them
Ye shall not be. . . .

And thou shalt be the first of witches known;
And thou shalt be the first of all i' the world;
And thou shalt teach the art of poisoning,
Of poisoning those who are great lords of all;
Yea, thou shalt make them die in their palaces;
And thou shalt bind the oppressor's soul (with power);[1]
And when ye find a peasant who is rich,
Then ye shall teach the witch, your pupil, how
To ruin all his crops with tempests dire,
With lightning and with thunder (terrible),
And with the hail and wind. . . .

[1] *Legare*, the binding and paralysing human faculties by means of witchcraft.

And when a priest shall do you injury
By his benedictions, ye shall do to him
Double the harm, and do it in the name
Of me, *Diana*, Queen of witches all!

And when the priests or the nobility
Shall say to you that you should put your faith
In the Father, Son, and Mary, then reply:
"Your God, the Father, and Maria are
Three devils. . . .

"For the true God the Father is not yours;
For I have come to sweep away the bad,
The men of evil, all will I destroy!

"Ye who are poor suffer with hunger keen,
And toil in wretchedness, and suffer too
Full oft imprisonment; yet with it all
Ye have a soul, and for your sufferings
Ye shall be happy in the other world,
But ill the fate of all who do ye wrong!"

Now when ARADIA had been taught, taught to work all witchcraft, how to destroy the evil race (of oppressors), she (imparted it to her pupils) and said unto them:

Quando io saro partita da questo mondo,
Qualunque cosa che avrete bisogna,
Una volta al mese quando la luna
E piena . . .
Dovete venire in luogo deserto,

In una selva tutte insieme,
E adorare lo spirito potente
Di mia madre *Diana*, e chi vorra
Imparare la stregonerie,
Che non la sopra,
Mia madre le insegnera,
Tutte cose. . . .
Sarete liberi dalla schiavitù !
E cosi diverrete tutti liberi !
Pero uomini e donne
Sarete tutti nudi, per fino.
Che non sara morto l' ultimo
Degli oppressori e morto,
Farete il giuoco della moccola
Di Benevento, e farete poi
Una cena cosi :

Translation

When I shall have departed from this world,
Whenever ye have need of anything,
Once in the month, and when the moon is full,
Ye shall assemble in some desert place,
Or in a forest all together join
To adore the potent spirit of your queen,
My mother, great *Diana*. She who fain
Would learn all sorcery yet has not won
Its deepest secrets, them my mother will
Teach her, in truth all things as yet unknown.
And ye shall all be freed from slavery,
And so ye shall be free in everything ;

And as the sign that ye are truly free,
Ye shall be naked in your rites, both men
And women also : this shall last until
The last of your oppressors shall be dead ;
And ye shall make the game of Benevento,
Extinguishing the lights, and after that
Shall hold your supper thus :

CHAPTER II

THE SABBAT, TREGUENDA OR WITCH-MEETING— HOW TO CONSECRATE THE SUPPER.

HERE follows the supper, of what it must consist, and what shall be said and done to consecrate it to DIANA.

You shall take meal and salt, honey and water, and make this incantation :

Scongiurazione alla Farina.

Scongiuro te, o farina!
Che sei il corpo nostro—senza di te
Non si potrebbe vivere—tu che
Prima di divenire la farina,
Sei stata sotto terra, dove tutti
Sono nascosti tutti in segreti,
Maccinata che siei a metterte al vento,
Tu spolveri per l' aria e te ne fuggi
Portando con te i tuoi segreti!

Ma quando grano sarai in spighe,
In spige belle che le lucciole,
Vengeno a farti lume perche tu
Possa crescere piú bella, altrimenti
Tu non potresti crescere a divenire bella,
Dunque anche tu appartieni

Alle Strege o alle Fate, perche
Le lucciole appartengono
Al sol. . . .
Lucciola caporala,
Vieni corri e vieni a gara,
Metti la briglia a la cavalla!
Metti la briglia al figluol del ré!
Vieni, corri e portala a mé!
Il figluol del ré te lasciera andare
Pero voglio te pigliare,
Giache siei bella e lucente,
Ti voglio mettere sotto un bicchiere
E guardarti colla lente;
Sotto un bicchiere tu staraí
Fino che tutti i segreti,
Di questo mondo e di quell' altro non mi farai
Sapere e anche quelle del grano,
E della farina appena,
Questi segreti io saprò,
Lucciola mia libera ti lascieró
Quando i segreti della terra io sapró
Tu sia benedetta ti diro!

Scongiurazione del Sale.

Scongiuro il sale suona mezza giòrno,
In punto in mezza a un fiume,
Entro e qui miro l' acqua,
L' acqua e al sol altro non penso,
Che a l' acqua e al sol, alloro
La mia mente tutta e rivolta,
Altra pensier non ho desidero,

Saper la verissima che tanto tempo é
Che soffro, vorrei saper il mio avenir,
Se cattivo fosse, acqua e sol
Migliorate il destino mio!

The Conjuration of Meal.

I conjure thee, O Meal!
Who art indeed our body, since without thee
We could not live, thou who (at first as seed)
Before becoming flower went in the earth,
Where all deep secrets hide, and then when ground
Didst dance like dust in the wind, and yet meanwhile
Didst bear with thee in flitting, secrets strange!

And yet erewhile, when thou wert in the ear,
Even as a (golden) glittering grain, even then
The fireflies came to cast on thee their light [1]
And aid thy growth, because without their help
Thou couldst not grow nor beautiful become;
Therefore thou dost belong unto the race
Of witches or of fairies, and because
The fireflies do belong unto the sun. . . .

. . . . . .

Queen of the Fireflies! hurry apace,[2]
Come to me now as if running a race,
Bridle the horse as you hear me now sing!
Bridle, O bridle the son of the king!
Come in a hurry and bring him to me!
The son of the king will ere long set thee free;

[1] There is an evident association here of the body of the firefly (which much resembles a grain of wheat) with the latter.

[2] The six lines following are often heard as a nursery rhyme.

And because thou for ever art brilliant and fair,
Under a glass I will keep thee ; while there,
With a lens I will study thy secrets concealed,
Till all their bright mysteries are fully revealed,
Yea, all the wondrous lore perplexed
Of this life of our cross and of the next.
Thus to all mysteries I shall attain,
Yea, even to that at last of the grain ;
And when this at last I shall truly know,
Firefly, freely I'll let thee go !
When Earth's dark secrets are known to me,
My blessing at last I will give to thee !

Here follows the Conjuration of the Salt.

Conjuration of the Salt.

I do conjure thee, salt, lo ! here at noon,
Exactly in the middle of a stream
I take my place and see the water round,
Likewise the sun, and think of nothing else
While here besides the water and the sun :
For all my soul is turned in truth to them ;
I do indeed desire no other thought,
I yearn to learn the very truth of truths,
For I have suffered long with the desire
To know my future or my coming fate,
If good or evil will prevail in it.
Water and sun, be gracious unto me !

Here follows the Conjuration of Cain.

Scongiurazione di Caïno.

Tuo Caïno, tu non possa aver
Ne pace e ne bene fino che
Dal sole[1] andate non sarai coi piedi
Correndo, le mani battendo,
E pregarlo per me che mi faccia sapere,
Il mio destino, se cattiva fosse,
Allora me lo faccia cambiare,
Se questa grazia mi farete,
L' acqua al lo splendor del sol la guardero:
E tu Caïno colla tua bocca mi dirai
Il mio destino quale sarà:
Se questa grazia o Caïno non mi farai,
Pace e bene non avrai!

The Conjuration of Cain.

I conjure thee, O Cain, as thou canst ne'er
Have rest or peace until thou shalt be freed
From the *sun* where thou art prisoned, and must go
Beating thy hands and running fast meanwhile:[2]
I pray thee let me know my destiny;
And if 'tis evil, change its course for me!
If thou wilt grant this grace, I'll see it clear
In the water in the splendour of the sun;
And thou, O Cain, shalt tell by word of mouth
Whatever this my destiny is to be.
And unless thou grantest this,
May'st thou ne'er know peace or bliss!

[1] Probably a mistake for *Luna*.

[2] This implies keeping himself warm, and is proof positive that *moon* should here be read for *sun*. According to another legend Cain suffers from cold in the moon.

Then shall follow the Conjuration of Diana.

Scongiurazione a Diana.

You shall make cakes of meal, wine, salt, and honey in the shape of a (crescent or horned) *moon*, and then put them to bake, and say:

Non cuoco ne il pane ne il sale,
Non cuoco ne il vino ne il miele,
Cuoco il corpo il sangue e l' anima,
L' anima di *Diana*, che non possa
Avere ne la pace e ne bene,
Possa essere sempre in mezzo alle pene
Fino che la grazia non mi farà,
Che glielo chiesta egliela chiedo di cuore!
Se questa grazia, o *Diana*, mi farai,
La cena in tua lode in molti la faremo,
Mangiaremo, beveremo,
Balleremo, salteremo,
Se questa grazia che ti ho chiesta,
Se questa grazia tu mi farai,
Nel tempo che balliamo,
Il lume spengnerai,
Cosi al l' amore
Liberamente la faremo!

Conjuration of Diana.

I do not bake the bread, nor with it salt,
Nor do I cook the honey with the wine;
I bake the body and the blood and soul,
The soul of (great) *Diana*, that she shall

Know neither rest nor peace, and ever be
In cruel suffering till she will grant
What I request, what I do most desire,
I beg it of her from my very heart!
And if the grace be granted, O *Diana!*
In honour of thee I will hold this feast,
Feast and drain the goblet deep,
We will dance and wildly leap,
And if thou grant'st the grace which I require,
Then when the dance is wildest, all the lamps
Shall be extinguished and we'll freely love!

And thus shall it be done: all shall sit down to the supper all naked, men and women, and, the feast over, they shall dance, sing, make music, and then love in the darkness, with all the lights extinguished; for it is the Spirit of *Diana* who extinguishes them, and so they will dance and make music in her praise.

And it came to pass that DIANA, after her daughter had accomplished her mission or spent her time on earth among the living (mortals), recalled her, and gave her the power that when she had been invoked . . . having done some good deed . . . she gave her the power to gratify those who had conjured her by granting her or him success in love:

To bless or curse with power friends or enemies [to do good or evil].

To converse with spirits.

To find hidden treasures in ancient ruins.

To conjure the spirits of priests who died leaving treasures.

To understand the voice of the wind.

To change water into wine.

To divine with cards.

To know the secrets of the hand (palmistry).

To cure diseases.

To make those who are ugly beautiful.

To tame wild beasts.

Whatever thing should be asked from the spirit of *Aradia*, that should be granted unto those who merited her favour.

And thus must they invoke her:

Thus do I seek Aradia! Aradia! Aradia![1] At midnight, at midnight I go into a field, and with me I bear water, wine, and salt, *I bear water, wine, and salt*, and my talisman—*my talisman, my talisman*, and a red small bag which I ever hold in my hand—*con dentro, con dentro, sale*, with salt in it, *in it*. With the water and wine I bless myself, *I bless myself* with devotion to implore a favour from Aradia, Aradia.

Scongiurazione di Aradia.

Aradia, Aradia mia!
Tu che siei figlia del più peggiore
Che si trova nell Inferno,
Che dal Paradiso fu discacciata,

[1] This is a formula which is to be slowly recited, emphasising the repetitions.

E con una sorella, te ha creata,
Ma tua madre pentita del suo fallo,
A voluto di fare di te uno spirito,
Un spirito benigno,
E non maligno!

Aradia, Aradia! Tanto ti prego
Per l' amore che por ti ha tua madre,
E a l' amor tuo che tanto l' ami,
Ti prego di farmi la grazia
La grazia che io ti chiedo
Se questa grazia mi farei,
Tre cose mi farai vedere,
    Serpe strisciare,
    Lucciola volare,
    E rana cantare
Se questa grazia non mi farai,
Desidero tu non possa avere,
Avere più pace e ne bene,
E che da lontano tu debba scomodarti.
E a me raccomodarti,
Che ti obri . . . che tu possa torrnar
Presto al tuo destino.

The Invocation to Aradia.

Aradia! my Aradia!
Thou who art daughter unto him who was
Most evil of all spirits, who of old
Once reigned in hell when driven away from heaven,
Who by his sister did thy sire become,
But as thy mother did repent her fault,

And wished to mate thee to a spirit who
Should be benevolent,
And not malevolent!

Aradia, Aradia! I implore
Thee by the love which she did bear for thee!
And by the love which I too feel for thee!
I pray thee grant the grace which I require!
And if this grace be granted, may there be
One of three signs distinctly clear to me:
        The hiss of a serpent,
        The light of a firefly,
        The sound of a frog!
But if you do refuse this favour, then
May you in future know no peace nor joy,
And be obliged to seek me from afar,
Until you come to grant me my desire,
In haste, and then thou may'st return again
Unto thy destiny. Therewith, Amen!

CHAPTER III

HOW DIANA MADE THE STARS AND THE RAIN

DIANA was the first created before all creation; in her were all things; out of herself, the first darkness, she divided herself; into darkness and light she was divided. Lucifer, her brother and son, herself and her other half, was the light.

And when *Diana* saw that the light was so beautiful, the light which was her other half, her brother Lucifer, she yearned for it with exceeding great desire. Wishing to receive the light again into her darkness, to swallow it up in rapture, in delight, she trembled with desire This desire was the Dawn.

But Lucifer, the light, fled from her, and would not yield to her wishes; he was the light which flies into the most distant parts of heaven, the mouse which flies before the cat.

Then *Diana* went to the fathers of the Beginning, to the mothers, the spirits who were before the first spirit, and lamented unto them that she could not prevail with Lucifer. And they praised her for her courage; they told her that to rise she must fall; to become the chief of goddesses she must become a mortal.

And in the ages, in the course of time, when the world was made, *Diana* went on earth, as did Lucifer, who had fallen, and *Diana* taught magic and sorcery, whence came witches and fairies and goblins—all that is like man, yet not mortal.

And it came thus that *Diana* took the form of a cat. Her brother had a cat whom he loved beyond all creatures, and it slept every night on his bed, a cat beautiful beyond all other creatures, a fairy: he did not know it.

Diana prevailed with the cat to change forms with her; so she lay with her brother, and in the darkness assumed her own form, and so by Lucifer became the mother of Aradia. But when in the morning he found that he lay by his sister, and that light had been conquered by darkness, Lucifer was extremely angry; but *Diana* sang to him a spell, a song of power, and he was silent, the song of the night which soothes to sleep; he could say nothing. So *Diana* with her wiles of witchcraft so charmed him that he yielded to her love. This was the first fascination; she hummed the song, it was as the buzzing of bees (or a top spinning round), a spinning-wheel spinning life. She spun the lives of all men; all things were spun from the wheel of *Diana*. Lucifer turned the wheel.

Diana was not known to the witches and spirits, the fairies and elves who dwell in desert place, the goblins, as their mother; she hid herself in humility and was a mortal, but by her will she rose again above all. She had such passion for witchcraft, and became so powerful therein, that her greatness could not be hidden.

And thus it came to pass one night, at the meeting of

all the sorceresses and fairies, she declared that she would darken the heavens and turn all the stars into mice.

All those who were present said—

"If thou canst do such a strange thing, having risen to such power, thou shalt be our queen."

Diana went into the street; she took the bladder of an ox and a piece of witch-money, which has an edge like a knife—with such money witches cut the earth from men's foot-tracks—and she cut the earth, and with it and many mice she filled the bladder, and blew into the bladder till it burst.

And there came a great marvel, for the earth which was in the bladder became the round heaven above, and for three days there was a great rain; the mice became stars or rain. And having made the heaven and the stars and the rain, *Diana* became Queen of the Witches; she was the cat who ruled the star-mice, the heaven and the rain.

CHAPTER IV

THE CHARM OF THE STONES CONSECRATED TO DIANA

To find a stone with a hole in it is a special sign of the favour of *Diana.* He who does so shall take it in his hand and repeat the following, having observed the ceremony as enjoined: —

Scongiurazione della pietra bucata.

Una pietra bucata
L' ho trovato;
Ne ringrazio il destin,
E lo spirito che su questa via
Mi ha portata,
Che passa essere il mio bene,
E la mia buona fortuna!

Mi alzo la mattina al alba,
E a passegio me ne vo
Nelle valli, monti e campi,
La fortuna cercarvo
Della ruta e la verbena,
Quello so porta fortuna

Me lo tengo in senno chiuso
E saperlo nessuno no le deve,
E cosi cio che commendo,
"La verbena far *ben* per me!
Benedica quella strege!
Quella fata che mi segna!"

Diana fu quella
Che mi venne la notte in sogno
E mi disse: "Se tu voir tener
Le cattive persone da te lontano,
Devi tenere sempre ruta con te,
Sempre ruta con te e verbena!"

Diana, tu che siei la regina
Del cielo e della terra e dell' inferno,
E siei la prottetrice degli infelici,
Dei ladri, degli assassini, e anche
Di donne di mali affari se hai conosciuto,
Che non sia stato l' indole cattivo
Delle persone, tu *Diana*,
Diana li hai fatti tutti felici!

Una altra volta ti scongiuro
Che tu non abbia ne pace ne bene,
Tu possa essere sempre in mezzo alle pene,
Fino che la grazia che io ti chiedo
Non mi farai!

Invocation to the Holy-Stone.[1]

I have found
A holy-stone upon the ground.
O Fate! I thank thee for the happy find,
Also the spirit who upon this road
Hath given it to me;
And may it prove to be for my true good
And my good fortune!

I rise in the morning by the earliest dawn,
And I go forth to walk through (pleasant) vales,
All in the mountains or the meadows fair,
Seeking for luck while onward still I roam,
Seeking for rue and vervain scented sweet,
Because they bring good fortune unto all.
I keep them safely guarded in my bosom,
That none may know it—'tis a secret thing,
And sacred too, and thus I speak the spell:
"O vervain! ever be a benefit,
And may thy blessing be upon the witch
Or on the fairy who did give thee to me!"

It was *Diana* who did come to me,
All in the night in a dream, and said to me:
"If thou would'st keep all evil folk afar,
Then ever keep the vervain and the rue
Safely beside thee!"

[1] Properly, the stone with a hole in it. But such a stone is called holy on shipboard, and here it has really a claim to the name.

Great *Diana!* thou
Who art the queen of heaven and of earth,
And of the infernal lands—yea, thou who art
Protectress of all men unfortunate,
Of thieves and murderers, and of women too
Who lead an evil life, and yet hast known
That their nature was not evil, thou, *Diana*,
Hast still conferred on them some joy in life.[1]

Or I may truly at another time
So conjure thee that thou shalt have no peace
Or happiness, for thou shalt ever be
In suffering until thou grantest that
Which I require in strictest faith from thee!

[Here we have again the threatening the deity, just as in Eskimo or other Shamanism, which represents the rudest primitive form of conjuring, the spirits are menaced. A trace of this is to be found among rude Roman Catholics. Thus when St. Bruno, some years ago, at a town in the Romagna, did not listen to the prayers of his devotees for rain, they stuck his image in the mud of the river, head downwards. A rain speedily followed, and the saint was restored in honour to his place in the church.]

[1] This is an obscure passage, but I believe that I have given it as the poet meant or felt it.

The Spell or Conjuration of the Round Stone.[1]

The finding a *round* stone, be it great or small, is a good sign (*e buono augurio*), but it should never be given away, because the receiver will then get the good luck, and some disaster befall the giver.

On finding a round stone, raise the eyes to heaven, and throw the stone up three times (catching it every time), and say :—

Spirito del buono augurio !
Sei venuto in mio soccorso,
Credi ne avevo gran bisogno,
Spirito del folletino rosso
Giacche sei venuto in mio soccorso,
Ti prego di non mi abbandonare !
Ti prego dentro questa palla d' intrare,
E nella mia tasca tu possa portare,
Cosi in qualunque mia bisogna,
In mio aiuto ti posso chiamare,
E di giorno e di notte,
Tu non mi possa abbandonare.

Se danari da qualchuno avanzerò,
E non mi vorra pagare,
Tu folletino rosso me li farei dare !
Si questo di non darmeli,
Si in testera tu vi anderai
E col tua *Briè—briè !*

[1] Il sasso a palla.

Se dorme lo desterai,
Panni dal letto laceraì,
Le farei tanta paura
Che allora di andare a dormire,
Andra alle bische a giuocare,
E tu nunqua lo seguirai.

E tu col tuo *Briè—briè*, le dirai,
Chi non paga deliti
Avranno pene e guai.

Cosi il debitare il giorno appresso
O mi portera i danari,
O me li mandera;
E cosi, folletino rosso!
Mi farai felice in mia vita,
Perche in qualcunque mia bisogna,
Verrai in mio soccorso!

Se colla mia amante saro' adirato,
Tu spirito del buono augurio mio!
Andrai la notte da lei
Per i capelli la prenderai,
E nel letto mio la porterai,
E la mattina quando tutti gli spiriti
Vanno a riposare,
Tu prima di si' entrare
Nella tua palla si porterai
La mia bella nel suo letto,
Cosi te prego, folletino,
Di entrare in questa mia palla!

E di ubbidire a tutti i miei commandi!
Ed io ti porteró
Sempre nella tasca mia,
Che tu non mi vada via.

The Conjuration.

Spirit of good omen,
Who art come to aid me,
Believe I had great need of thee.
Spirit of the Red Goblin,
Since thou hast come to aid me in my need,
I pray of thee do not abandon me:
I beg of thee to enter now this stone,
That in my pocket I may carry thee,
And so when anything is needed by me,
I can call unto thee: be what it may,
Do not abandon me by night or day.

Should I lend money unto any man
Who will not pay when due, I pray of thee,
Thou the Red Goblin, make him pay his debt!
And if he will not and is obstinate,
Go at him with thy cry of "*Brié—brié!*"
And if he sleeps, awake him with a twitch,
And pull the covering off and frighten him!
And follow him about where'er he goes.

So teach him with thy ceaseless "*Brie—brie!*"
That he who obligation e'er forgets
Shall be in trouble till he pays his debts.

And so my debtor on the following day
Shall either bring the money which he owes,
Or send it promptly: so I pray of thee,
O my Red Goblin, come unto my aid!
Or should I quarrel with her whom I love,
Then, spirit of good luck, I pray thee go
To her while sleeping—pull her by the hair,
And bear her through the night unto my bed!
And in the morning, when all spirits go
To their repose, do thou, ere thou return'st
Into thy stone, carry her home again,
And leave her there asleep. Therefore, O Sprite!
I beg thee in this pebble make thy home!
Obey in every way all I command.
So in my pocket thou shalt ever be,
And thou and I will ne'er part company!

CHAPTER V

THE CONJURATION OF THE LEMON AND PINS

Scongiurazione al Limone appuntato un Spille.

Sacred to Diana.

A lemon stuck full of pins of different colours always brings good fortune.

If you receive as a gift a lemon full of pins of divers colours, without any black ones among them, it signifies that your life will be perfectly happy and prosperous and joyful.

But if some black pins are among them, you may enjoy good fortune and health, yet mingled with troubles which may be of small account. [However, to lessen their influence, you must perform the following ceremony, and pronounce this incantation, wherein all is also described.[1]]

The Incantation to Diana.

Al punto di mezza notte
Un limone ho raccolto,
Lo raccolto nel giardino
Ho raccolto un limone,

[1] This passage is not given in the original MS., but it is necessary to clearly explain what follows abruptly.

Un arancio e un mandarino,
Cogliendo queste cose,
Cogliendo, io ho detto;
Tu, o Regina del sole
Della luna e delle stelle,
Ti chiamo in mio ajuto
E con quanta forza ho a te scongiuro
Che una grazia tu mi voglia fare,
Tre cose ho racolto nel giardino;
Un limone, un arancio,
E un mandarino; una
Di queste cose per mia fortuna,
Voglio tenere due
Di questi oggetti di mano,
E quello chi dovra servirmi
Per la buona fortuna
Regina delle stelle:
Fa lo rimanere in mia mano!

At the instant when the midnight came,
I have picked a lemon in the garden,
I have picked a lemon, and with it
An orange and a (fragrant) mandarin.
Gathering with care these (precious) things,
And while gathering I said with care:
"Thou who art Queen of the sun and of the moon
And of the stars—lo! here I call to thee!
And with what power I have I conjure thee
To grant to me the favour I implore!
Three things I've gathered in the garden here:

A lemon, orange, and a mandarin;
I've gathered them to bring good luck to me.
Two of them I do grasp here in my hand,
And that which is to serve me for my fate,
Queen of the stars!
Then make that fruit remain firm in my grasp.

[Something is here omitted in the MS. I conjecture that the two are tossed without seeing them into the air, and if the lemon remains, the ceremony proceeds as follows. This is evident, since in it the incantation is confused with a prose direction how to act.]

Saying this, one looks up at the sky, and I found the lemon in one hand, and a voice said to me—

"Take many pins, and carefully stick them in the lemon, pins of many colours; and as thou wilt have good luck, and if thou desirest to give the lemon to any one or to a friend, thou shouldst stick in it many pins of varied colours.

"But if thou wilt that evil befall any one, put in it black pins.

"But for this thou must pronounce a different incantation (thus)":—

Dia *Diana*, a te scongiuro!
E te chiamo ad alta voce!
Che tu non abbia pace ne bene
Se non viene in mio aiuto

Domani al punto di mezzo giorno,
Ti aspetto a quello punto
Un bicchiere di vino portero,
E una piccola lente al occhio
E dentro tredeci spilli,
Spilli neri vi metterò,
E tu *Diana* tutti
I diavoli dell' inferno chiamerai,
E in compagnia del sole li manderai,
E tutto il fuoco dell' inferno preso di se
Lo porteranno, e daranno forza
Al sole di farmi questo vino bollire,
Perche questi spilli possano arroventire,
E con questi il limone apunteró
Per non dare più pace,
E ne bene alla persona
Che questo limone le presenterò !

Se questa grazia mi farete,
Un segnale mi darete,
Dentro tre giorni,
Una cosa voglio vedere,
O vento, o acqua, o grandine,
Se questo segnale non avró,
Piu pace *Diana* non te darò,
Tanto di giorno che di notte,
Sempre ti tormenterò.

The Invocation to Diana.

Goddess *Diana*, I do conjure thee
And with uplifted voice to thee I call,
That thou shalt never have content or peace
Until thou comest to give me all thy aid.
Therefore to-morrow at the stroke of noon
I'll wait for thee, bearing a cup of wine,
Therewith a lens or a small burning-glass.[1]
And thirteen pins I'll put into the charm;
Those which I put shall all indeed be black,
But thou, *Diana*, thou wilt place them all!

And thou shalt call for me the fiends from hell;
Thou'lt send them as companions of the Sun,
And all the fire infernal of itself
Those fiends shall bring, and bring with it the power
Unto the Sun to make this (red) wine boil,[2]
So that these pins by heat may be red-hot;
And with them I do fill the lemon here,
That unto her or him to whom 'tis given
Peace and prosperity shall be unknown.

If this grace I gain from thee
Give a sign, I pray, to me!

[1] This appears from very early ages, as in Roman times, to have been regarded as gifted with magic properties, and was used in occult ceremonies.

[2] That is, *Diana* is invoked to send demons with the very life of the fire of hell to still more increase that of the sun to intensify the wine.

C

Ere the third day
Shall pass away,
Let me either hear or see
A roaring wind, a rattling rain,
Or hail a clattering on the plain;
Till one of these three signs you show,
Peace, *Diana*, thou shalt not know.
Answer well the prayer I've sent thee,
Or day and night will I torment thee!

As the orange was the fruit of the Sun, so is the lemon suggestive of the Moon or Diana, its colour being of a lighter yellow. However, the lemon specially chosen for the charm is always a green one, because it "sets hard" and turns black. It is not generally known that orange and lemon peel, subjected to pressure and combined with an adhesive may be made into a hard substance which can be moulded or used for many purposes. I have devoted a chapter to this in an as yet unpublished work entitled *One Hundred Minor Arts*. This was suggested to me by the hardened lemon given to me for a charm by a witch.

CHAPTER VI

A SPELL TO WIN LOVE

When a wizard, a worshipper of *Diana*, one who worships the Moon, desires the love of a woman, he can change her into the form of a dog, when she, forgetting who she is, and all things besides, will at once come to his house, and there, when by him, take on again her natural form and remain with him. And when it is time for her to depart, she will again become a dog and go home, where she will turn into a girl. And she will remember nothing of what has taken place, or at least but little or mere fragments, which will seem as a confused dream. And she will take the form of a dog because *Diana* has ever a dog by her side.

And this is the spell to be repeated by him who would bring a love to his home.[1]

To day is Friday, and I wish to rise very early, not having been able to sleep all night, having seen a very beautiful girl, the daughter of a rich lord, whom I dare not hope to win. Were she poor, I could gain her with money; but as she is rich, I have no hope to do so. (Therefore will I conjure *Diana* to aid me.)

---

1 The beginning of this spell seems to be merely a prose introduction explaining the nature of the ceremony.

Scongiurazione a Diana.

Diana, bella Diana!
Che tanto bella e buona siei,
E tanto ti é piacere
Ti ho fatto,
Anche a te di fare al amore,
Dunque spero che anche in questa cosa
Tu mi voglia aiutare,
E se tu vorrai
Tutto tu potrai,
Se questa grazia mi vorrai fare:
Chiamerai tua figlia *Aradia*,
Al letto della bella fanciulla
La mandera *Aradia*,
La fanciulla in una canina convertira,
Alla camera mia la mandera,
Ma entrata in camera mia,
Non sara più una canina,
Ma tornerà una bella fanciulla,
Bella cane era prima,
E cosi potrò fare al amore
A mio piacimento,
Come a me piacera.
Quando mi saro divertito
A mi piacere dirò.
"Per volere della Fata Diana,
E di sua figlia Aradia,
Torna una canina
Come tu eri prima!"

Invocation to Diana.

DIANA, beautiful DIANA!
Who art indeed as good as beautiful,
By all the worship I have given thee,
And all the joy of love which thou hast known,
I do implore thee aid me in my love!
    What thou wilt 'tis true
    Thou canst ever do:
And if the grace I seek thou'lt grant to me,
Then call, I pray, thy daughter ARADIA,
And send her to the bedside of the girl,
And give that girl the likeness of a dog,
And make her then come to me in my room,
But when she once has entered it, I pray
That she may reassume her human form,
As beautiful as e'er she was before,
And may I then make love to her until
Our souls with joy are fully satisfied.
Then by the aid of the great Fairy Queen
And of her daughter, fair *Aradia*,
May she be turned into a dog again,
And then to human form as once before!

Thus it will come to pass that the girl as a dog will return to her home unseen and unsuspected, for thus will it be effected by Aradia; and the girl will think it is all a dream, because she will have been enchanted by ARADIA.

CHAPTER VII

TO FIND OR BUY ANYTHING, OR TO HAVE GOOD FORTUNE THEREBY

An Invocation or Incantation to Diana.

THE man or woman who, when about to go forth into the town, would fain be free from danger or risk of an accident : or to have good fortune in *buying*, as, for instance, if a scholar hopes that he may find some rare old book or manuscript for sale very cheaply, or if any one wishes to buy anything very desirable or to find bargains or rarities. This *scongiurazione* serves for good health, cheerfulness of heart, and absence of evil or the overcoming enmity. These are words of gold unto the believer.

The Invocation.

Siamo di Martedi e a buon ora
Mi voglio levare la buona fortuna,
Voglio andare e cercare,
E coll aiuto della bella *Diana*,
La voglio trovare prima d' andare,
Prima di sortir di casa
Il malocchio mi levero

Con tre gocciole d' olio,[1]
E te bella *Diana* io invoco
Che tu possa mandarmi via
Il malocchio da dosse a me
E mandala al mio più nemico!

Quando il malocchio
Mi saro levato
In mezza alla via lo gettero,
Se questa grazia mi farei
Diana bella,
Tutti i campanelli
Di mia casa bene suonerai,
Allora contento di casa me ne andro,
Perche col tuo aiuto (saro) certo di trovare,
Buona fortuna, certo di trovare
Un bel libro antico,
E a buon mercato
Me lo farai comprare!

Tu stessa dal proprietario
Che avra il libro
Te ne andrai tu stessa
Lo troverai e lo farei,

1 This refers to a small ceremony which I have seen performed scores of times, and have indeed had it performed over me almost as often, as an act of courtesy common among wizards and witches. It consists of making certain signs and crosses over a few drops of oil and the head of the one blessed, accompanied by a short incantation. I have had the ceremony seriously commended or prescribed to me as a means of keeping in good health and prosperity.

Capitare in mano al padrone,
E le farai capitare
In mano al padrone,
E le farai entrare
Nel cervello che se di quel libro
Non si disfara la scomunica,
Le portera, cosi questo dell' libro,
Verra disfarsi e col tuo aiuto,
Verra portato alla mia presenza,
E a poco me lo vendera,
Oppure se e' un *manoscritto*,
Invece di libro per via lo gettera,
E col tuo aiuto verra in mia presenza,
E potrò acquistarlo
Senza nessuna spesa;
E cosi per me
Sara grande fortuna!

To Diana.

'Tis Tuesday now, and at an early hour
I fain would turn good fortune to myself,
Firstly at home and then when I go forth,
And with the aid of beautiful *Diana*
I pray for luck ere I do leave this house!

First with three drops of oil I do remove
All evil influence, and I humbly pray,
O beautiful *Diana*, unto thee
That thou wilt take it all away from me,
And send it all to my worst enemy!

When the evil fortune
Is taken from me,
I'll cast it out to the middle of the street :
And if thou wilt grant me this favour,
O beautiful *Diana*,
Every bell in my house shall merrily ring !

Then well contented
I will go forth to roam,
Because I shall be sure that with thy aid
I shall discover ere I return
Some fine and ancient books,
And at a moderate price.

And thou shalt find the man,
The one who owns the book,
And thou thyself wilt go
And put it in his mind,
Inspiring him to know
What 'tis that thou would'st find
And move him into doing
All that thou dost require.
Or if a manuscript
Written in ancient days,
Thou'lt gain it all the same,
It shall come in thy way,
And thus at little cost.
Thou shalt buy what thou wilt,
By great *Diana's* aid.

The foregoing was obtained, after some delay, in reply to a query as to what conjuration would be required before going forth, to make sure that one should find for sale some rare book, or other object desired, at a very moderate price. Therefore the invocation has been so worded as to make it applicable to literary finds; but those who wish to buy anything whatever on equally favourable terms, have but to vary the request, retaining the introduction, in which the magic virtue consists. I cannot, however, resist the conviction that it is most applicable to, and will succeed best with, researches for objects of antiquity, scholarship, and art, and it should accordingly be deeply impressed on the memory of every bric-à-brac hunter and bibliographer. It should be observed, and that earnestly, that the prayer, far from being answered, will turn to the contrary or misfortune, unless the one who repeats it does so in fullest faith, and this cannot be acquired by merely saying to oneself, "I believe." For to acquire real faith in anything requires long and serious mental discipline, there being, in fact, no subject which is so generally spoken of and so little understood. Here, indeed, I am speaking seriously, for the man who can train his faith to actually believe in and cultivate or develop his will can really work what the world by common consent regards as miracles. A time will come when this principle will form not only the basis of all education, but also that of all moral and social culture. I have, I trust, fully set it forth in a work entitled "Have you a Strong Will? or how to Develop it or any other Faculty or Attribute of the Mind, and render it Habitual," &c. London: GEORGE REDWAY.

The reader, however, who has devout faith, can, as the witches declare, apply this spell daily before going forth to procuring or obtaining any kind of bargains at shops, to picking up or discovering lost objects, or, in fact, to finds of any kind. If he incline to beauty in female form, he will meet with *bonnes fortunes;* if a man of business, bargains will be his. The botanist who repeats it before going into the fields will probably discover some new plant, and the astronomer by night be almost certain to run against a brand-new planet, or at least an asteroid. It should be repeated before going to the races, to visit friends, places of amusement, to buy or sell, to make speeches, and specially before hunting or any nocturnal goings-forth, since *Diana* is the goddess of the chase and of night. But woe to him who does it for a jest!

CHAPTER VIII

TO HAVE A GOOD VINTAGE AND VERY GOOD WINE BY THE AID OF DIANA

" Sweet is the vintage when the showering grapes
In Bacchanal profusion reel to earth,
Purple and gushing."

—BYRON, *Don Juan*, c. 124.

" Vinum bonum et suave,
Bonis bonum, pravis prave,
O quam dulcis sapor—ave!
Mundana lætitia!"

—*Latin Songs*, E. DU MERIL.

HE who would have a good vintage and fine wine, should take a *horn* full of wine and with this go into the vineyards or farms wherever vines grow, and then drinking from the horn, say :—

Bevo ma non bevo il vino,
Bevo il sangue di *Diana*,
Che da vino nel sangue di *Diana*
Si deve convertire,
E in tutte le mie viti
Lo spandera,
E buona raccolta mi verra
E quando avro avuto buona raccolta,

Non saro ancora fuori di sciagura,
Perche il vino cattivo mi puol venire
Perche puol nascere l' uva
A luna vecchia . . .
E cosi il mio vino puole sempre andare
In malora—ma io bevendo
In questo corno, e bevendo il sangue,
Il sangue di *Diana* col suo aiuto
La mano alla Luna nuova io bacero,
Che la mia uva possa guardare,
Al momento che crea l' occhiolo
Alla Crescenza del uva
E fino alla raccolta,
Che possa venire il mio vino buono,
E che si possa mantenere
Da prendere molti quattrini,
E possa entrare la buona fortuna
Nelle mi e vigne,
E nei miei poderi !

Quando il mio vino pendera
Di andare a male, il corno prendero,
E forte, forte lo suonero,
Nel punto della mezza notte,
Dentro alla mia cantina lo suonero,
Lo suonero tanto forte
Che tu bella *Diana* anche da molto lontano,
Tu lo possa sentire,
E finestre e porte
Con gran forza tu possa spalancare,

A gran corsa tu mi possa venire,
A trovare, e tu possa salvarmi
Il mio vino, e tu possa salvare,
Salvare me da grande sciagura,
Perche se il mio vino a male andera
La miseria mi prendera.
E col tuo aiuto bella *Diana*,
Io saro salvato.

I drink, and yet it is not wine I drink,
I drink the blood of *Diana*,
Since from wine it has changed into her blood,
And spread itself through all my growing vines,
Whence it will give me good return in wines,
Though even if good vintage should be mine,
I'll not be free from care, for should it chance
That the grape ripens in the waning moon,
Then all the wine would come to sorrow, but
If drinking from this horn I drink the blood—
The blood of great *Diana*—by her aid—
If I do kiss my hand to the new moon,
Praying the Queen that she will guard my grapes,
Even from the instant when the bud is born
Until it is a ripe and perfect grape,
And onward to the vintage, and to the last
Until the wine is made—may it be good!
And may it so succeed that I from it
May draw good profit when at last 'tis sold,
So may good fortune come unto my vines,
And into all my land where'er it be!

But should my vines seem in an evil way,
I'll take my horn, and bravely will I blow
In the wine-vault at midnight, and I'll make
Such a tremendous and a terrible sound
That thou, *Diana* fair, however far
Away thou may'st be, still shalt hear the call,
And casting open door or window wide,
Shalt headlong come upon the rushing wind,
And find and save me—that is, save my vines,
Which will be saving me from dire distress;
For should I lose them I'd be lost myself,
But with thy aid, *Diana*, I'll *be saved.*

[This is a very interesting invocation and tradition, and probably of great antiquity from very striking intrinsic evidence. For it is firstly devoted to a subject which has received little attention—the connection of Diana as the moon with Bacchus, although in the great *Dizionario Storico Mitologico*, by Pozzoli and others, it is expressly asserted that in Greece her worship was associated with that of Bacchus, Esculapius, and Apollo. The connecting link is the *horn*. In a medal of Alexander Severus, Diana of Ephesus bears the horn of plenty. This is the horn or horns of the new moon, sacred to Diana. According to Callimachus, Apollo himself built an altar consisting entirely of horns to *Diana*.

The connection of the horn with wine is

obvious. It was usual among the old Slavonians for the priest of Svantevit, the Sun-god, to see if the horn which the idol held in his hand was full of wine, in order to prophesy a good harvest for the coming year. If it was filled, all was right; if not, he filled the horn, drank from it, and replaced the horn in the hand, and predicted that all would eventually go well.[1] It cannot fail to strike the reader that this ceremony is strangely like that of the Italian invocation, the only difference being that in one the Sun, and in the other the Moon is invoked to secure a good harvest.

In the *Legends of Florence* there is one of the Via del Corno, in which the hero, falling into a vast tun or *tina* of wine, is saved from drowning by sounding a horn with tremendous power. At the sound, which penetrates to an incredible distance, even to unknown lands, all come rushing as if enchanted to save him. In this conjuration, *Diana*, in the depths of heaven, is represented as rushing at the sound of the horn, and leaping through doors or windows to save the vintage of the one who blows. There is a certain singular affinity in these stories.

In the story of the *Via del Corno*, the hero is

[1] KREUSSLER, *Sorbenwendische Alterthümer*, Pt. I. p. 272.

saved by the Red Goblin or Robin Goodfellow, who gives him a horn, and it is the same sprite who appears in the conjuration of the Round Stone, which is sacred to Diana. This is because the spirit is nocturnal, and attendant on Diana-Titania.

Kissing the hand to the new moon is a ceremony of unknown antiquity, and JOB, even in his time, regarded it as heathenish and forbidden — which always means antiquated and out of fashion—as when he declared (xxxi. 26, 27), "If I beheld the moon walking in brightness . . . and my heart hath been secretly enticed or my mouth hath kissed my hand . . . this also were an iniquity to be punished by the Judge, for I should have denied the God that is above." From which it may or ought to be inferred that Job did not understand that God made the moon and appeared in all His works, or else he really believed the moon was an independent deity. In any case, it is curious to see the old forbidden rite still living, and as heretical as ever.

The tradition, as given to me, very evidently omits a part of the ceremony, which may be supplied from classic authority. When the peasant performs the rite, he must not act as once a certain African, who was a servant of a friend of mine, did. The coloured man's duty was to pour out every morning a libation of rum to a fetish—and he poured it down his own throat. The peasant should also sprinkle the vines, just as the Devonshire farmers, who observed all Christmas ceremonies, sprinkled, also from a horn, their apple-trees.

CHAPTER IX

TANA AND ENDAMONE, OR DIANA AND ENDYMION

"Hic ultra Endymionem indormit negligentiæ."

"Now it is fabled that Endymion, admitted to Olympus, whence he was expelled for want of respect to Juno, was banished for thirty years to earth. And having been allowed to sleep this time in a cave of Mount Latmos, *Diana*, smitten with his beauty, visited him every night till she had by him fifty daughters and one son. And after this Endymion was recalled to Olympus."

—*Diz. Stor. Mitol.*

THE following legend and the spells were given under the name or title of TANA. This was the old Etruscan name for *Diana*, which is still preserved in the Romagna Toscana. In more than one Italian and French work I have found some account or tale how a witch charmed a girl to sleep for a lover, but this is the only explanation of the whole ceremony known to me.

TANA.

Tana is a beautiful goddess, and she loved a marvellously handsome youth named Endamone; but her love was crossed by a witch who was her rival, although Endamone did not care for the latter.

But the witch resolved to win him, whether he would

or not, and with this intent she induced the servant of Endamone to let her pass the night in the latter's room. And when there, she assumed the appearance of Tana, whom he loved, so that he was delighted to behold her, as he thought, and welcomed her with passionate embraces. Yet this gave him into her power, for it enabled her to perform a certain magic spell by clipping a lock of his hair.[1]

Then she went home, and taking a piece of sheep's intestine, formed of it a purse, and in this she put that which she had taken, with a red and a black ribbon bound together, with a feather, and pepper and salt, and then sang a song. These were the words, a song of witchcraft of the very old time.

Scongiurazione.

Ho formato questo sachetto a Endamone,
E la mia vendetta per l' amore,
Ch'io ti portavo, e non ero corrisposta,
Una altra tu l' amavi :
La bella dea Tana tu amavi,
E tu non l' avrai : di passione
Ti struggerai, volonta di fare,
Di fare al amore tu avrai,

[1] According to all evil witchcraft in the world — especially among the black Voodoos — any individual can be injured or killed if the magician can obtain any portion of the *person*, however small, especially a lock of hair. This is specially described in *Thiodolf the Islander*, a romance by La Motte Fouqué. The exchange of locks by lovers is possibly connected with magic.

E non la potrai fare. Sempre addormentato
resterai,
Di un sonno che tutto sentirai,
E la tua bella tu vedrai,
Ma parlare non potrai
Nel vedere la tua bella,
Volontà di fare al amore
Verra e non la potrai fare
Come una candela ti struggera,
Ti struggererai poco a poco,
Come una candele a fuoco,
Tu non potrai vivère,
Tu non potrai stare,
Ti sentirai mancare,
Che il tuo cuore ritto sempre possa stare
E al amore più non potrai fare
Per l' amore che io te ho portata vo,
Sia convertito intanto odio
Che questo Endamone e la mia vendetta,
E cosi sono contenta.

The Spell.

This bag for Endamon' I wove,
It is my vengeance for the love,
For the deep love I had for thee,
Which thou would'st not return to me,
But bore it all to Tana's shrine,
And Tana never shall be thine!
Now every night in agony
By me thou shalt oppressed be!

From day to day, from hour to hour,
I'll make thee feel the witch's power;
With passion thou shalt be tormented,
And yet with pleasure ne'er contented;
Enwrapped in slumber thou shalt lie,
To know that thy beloved is by,
And, ever dying, never die,
Without the power to speak a word,
Nor shall her voice by thee be heard;
Tormented by Love's agony,
There shall be no relief for thee!
For my strong spell thou canst not break,
And from that sleep thou ne'er shalt wake:
Little by little thou shalt waste,
Like taper by the embers placed.
Little by little thou shalt die,
Yet, ever living, tortured lie,
Strong in desire, yet ever weak,
Without the power to move or speak,
With all the love I had for thee
Shalt thou thyself tormented be,
Since all the love I felt of late
I'll make thee feel in burning hate,
For ever on thy torture bent,
I am revenged, and now content.

But Tana, who was far more powerful than the witch, though not able to break the spell by which he was compelled to sleep, took from him all pain (he knew her in dreams), and embracing him, she sang this counter-charm.

The Song of Diana.

Endamone, Endamone, Endamone!
Per l' amore chi mi porti e che io pure,
Ti porto tre croci su questo letto!
Vengo a fare, e tre marroni d' India,
Nel tuo letto vengo a posare,
E questa finestra aperta che la Luna,
Su il tuo letto risplende,
Come risplende il nostro amore
La, e la prego con gran calore,
Che voglia dare sfogo a queste due cuore,
Che tanto ci amiano, e se questa grazia,
Mi verrà fatta chiunque sia innamorata,
Se mi scongiurera
In suo aiuto correro!

Endamone, Endamone, Endamone!
Sopra te io mi metto al lume,
Il tuo (cuore) lo dimeno,
E mi dimeno io pure e cosi,
E cosi tanto farò,
Tanto farò e tanto faremmo,
Che uniti ne veremmo.

The Counter-Charm.

Endamone, Endamone, Endamone!
By the love I feel, which I
Shall ever feel until I die,

Three crosses on thy bed I make,
And then three wild horse-chestnuts take;[1]
In that bed the nuts I hide,
And then the window open wide,
That the full moon may cast her light
Upon a love as fair and bright,
And so I pray to her above
To give wild rapture to our love,
And cast her fire in either heart,
Which wildly loves to never part;
And one thing more I beg of thee!
If any one enamoured be,
And in my aid his love hath placed,
Unto his call I'll come in haste.

So it came to pass that the fair goddess made love with Endamone as if they had been awake (yet communing in dreams). And so it is to this day, that whoever would make love with him or her who sleeps, should have recourse to the beautiful *Tana*, and so doing there will be success.

This legend, while agreeing in many details with the classical myth, is strangely intermingled with practices of witchcraft, but even these, if investigated, would all prove to be as ancient as the rest of the text. Thus the sheep's intestine —used instead of the red woollen bag which is

[1] *Marroni d' India.* A strong charm against evil, hence frequently carried against rheumatism, &c. The three should come from one shell.

employed in beneficent magic—the red and black ribbon, which mingles threads of joy and woe—the (peacock's) feather or *la penna maligna*—pepper and salt, occur in many other incantations, but always to bring evil and cause suffering.[1]

I have never seen it observed, but it is true, that KEATS in his exquisite poem of *Endymion* completely departs from or ignores the whole spirit and meaning of the ancient myth, while in this rude witch-song it is minutely developed. The conception is that of a beautiful youth furtively kissed in his slumber by *Dian* of reputed chastity. The ancient myth is, to begin with, one of darkness and light, or day and night, from which are born the fifty-one (now fifty-two) weeks of the year. This is *Diana*, the night, and Apollo, the sun, or light in another form. It is expressed as love-making during sleep, which, when it occurs in real life, generally has for active agent some one who, without being absolutely modest, wishes to preserve appearances. The established character of *Diana* among the Initiated (for which she was bitterly reviled by the Fathers of the Church) was that of a beautiful hypocrite who pursued amours in silent secrecy.

> "Thus as the moon Endymion lay with her,
> So did Hippolytus and Verbio."

1 The reader will find them described in my *Etrusco-Roman Remains*.

(On which the reader may consult TERTULLIAN, *De Falsa Religione*, lib. ii. cap. 17, and PICO DE MIRANDULA, *La Strega.*)

But there is an exquisitely subtle, delicately strange idea or ideal in the conception of the apparently chaste "clear cold moon" casting her living light by stealth into the hidden recesses of darkness and acting in the occult mysteries of love or dreams. So it struck BYRON [1] as an original thought that the sun does not shine on half the forbidden deeds which the moon witnesses, and this is emphasised in the Italian witch-poem. In it the moon is distinctly invoked as the protectress of a strange and secret amour, and as the deity to be especially invoked for such love-making. The one invoking says that the window is opened, that the moon may shine splendidly on the bed, even as our love is bright and beautiful . . . and I pray her to give great rapture—*sfogo*—to us.

The quivering, mysteriously beautiful light of the moon, which seems to cast a spirit of intelligence or emotion over silent Nature, and dimly

[1] "The sun set and uprose the yellow moon :
The devil's in the moon for mischief ; they
Who called her chaste, methinks, began too soon
Their nomenclature ; there is not a day
The longest, not the twenty-first of June,
Sees half the business in a wicked way
On which three single hours of moonshine smile."

—*Don Juan*, cxiii.

half awaken it—raising shadows into thoughts and causing every tree and rock to assume the semblance of a living form, but one which, while shimmering and breathing, still sleeps in a dream—could not escape the Greeks, and they expressed it as Diana embracing Endymion. But as night is the time sacred to secrecy, and as the true Diana of the Mysteries was the Queen of Night, who wore the crescent moon, and mistress of all hidden things, including "sweet secret sins and loved iniquities," there was attached to this myth far more than meets the eye. And just in the degree to which *Diana* was believed to be Queen of the emancipated witches and of Night, or the nocturnal Venus-Astarte herself, so far would the love for the sleeping Endymion be understood as sensual, yet sacred and allegorical. And it is entirely in this sense that the witches in Italy, who may claim with some right to be its true inheritors, have preserved and understood the myth.

It is a *realisation* of forbidden or secret love, with attraction to the dimly seen beautiful-by-moonlight, with the fairy or witch-like charm of the supernatural—a *romance* all combined in a single strange form—the spell of Night!

"There is a dangerous silence in that hour,
A stillness which leaves room for the full soul
To open all itself, without the power
Of calling wholly back its self-control;

CHAPTER X

MADONNA DIANA

"The Madonna is essentially the goddess of the moon."
—"*Naples in the Nineties*," by E. N. Rolfe.

Once there was, in the very old time in Cettardo Alto, a girl of astonishing beauty, and she was betrothed to a young man who was as remarkable for good looks as herself; but though well born and bred, the fortune or misfortunes of war or fate had made them both extremely poor. And if the young lady had one fault, it was her great pride, nor would she willingly be married unless in good style, with luxury and festivity, in a fine garment, with many bridesmaids of rank.

And this became to the beautiful *Rorasa*—for such was her name—such an object of desire, that her head was half turned with it, and the other girls of her acquaintance, to say nothing of the many men whom she had refused, mocked her so bitterly, asking her when the fine wedding was to be, with many other jeers and sneers, that at last in a moment of madness she went to the top of a high tower, whence she cast herself; and to make it worse, there was below a terrible ravine (*balza*), into which she fell.

Yet she took no harm, for as she fell there appeared to her a very beautiful woman, truly not of earth, who took her by the hand and bore her through the air to a safe place.

Then all the people round about who saw or heard of this thing cried out, "Lo, a miracle!" and they came and made a great festival, and would fain persuade Rorasa that she had been saved by the Madonna.

But the lady who had saved her, coming to her secretly, said: "If thou hast any desire, follow the Gospel of *Diana*, or what is called the Gospel of the Witches (*Il Vangelo delle Strege*), who worship the moon."

"Se la Luna adorerai
Tutto tu otterai."

"If thou adorest Luna, then
What thou desir'st thou shalt obtain!"

Then the beautiful girl went forth alone by night to the fields, and kneeling on a stone in an old ruin, she worshipped the moon and invoked *Diana* thus:—

DIANA, bella *Diana!*
Tu che della grande caduta
Mi ai bene salvata!
Ti prego di farmi una altra grazia,
Di farmi far' un bello sposalizio,
Una sposalizio ricco e 'compagnato
Da molte signore . . .
Se questa grazia mi farai
Sempre il Vangelo delle Strege
Io asseriro.

DIANA, beautiful *Diana!*
Thou who didst save from a dreadful death
When I did fall into the dark ravine!
I pray thee grant me still another grace.
Give me one glorious wedding, and with it
Full many bridesmaids, beautiful and grand;
And if this favour thou wilt grant to me,
True to the Witches' Gospel I will be!

When Rorasa awoke in the morning, she found herself in another house, where all was far more magnificent, and having risen, a beautiful maid led her into another room, where she was dressed in a superb wedding-garment of white silk with diamonds, for it was her wedding-dress indeed. Then there appeared ten young ladies, all splendidly attired, and with them and many distinguished persons she went to the church in a carriage. And all the streets were filled with music and people bearing flowers.

So she found the bridegroom, and was wedded to her heart's desire, ten times more grandly than she had ever dreamed of. Then, after the ceremony, there was spread a feast at which all the nobility of Cettardo were present, and, moreover, the whole town, rich and poor, were feasted.

When the wedding was finished, the bridesmaids made every one a magnificent present to the bride—one gave diamonds, another a parchment (written) in gold, after which they asked permission to go all together into the sacristy. And there they remained for some hours undisturbed, till the priest sent his *chierico* to inquire whether they wanted anything. But what was the youth's amazement at beholding, not the ten bridesmaids, but their ten images or likenesses in wood and in terra-cotta, with that of DIANA standing on a moon, and they were all so magnificently made and adorned as to be of immense value.

Therefore the priest put these images into the church, which is the most ancient in Cettardo, and now in many churches you may see the Madonna and Moon, but it is Diana—*la Dea della Luna*. The name Rorasa seems to indicate the Latin *ros* the dew, rorare, to bedew, *rorulenta*, bedewed—in fact, the goddess of the dew. Her great fall and being lifted by Diana suggest the fall of dew by night, and its rising in vapour under the influence of the moon. It is possible that this is a very old Latin mythic tale. The white silk and diamonds indicate the dew.

CHAPTER XI

THE HOUSE OF THE WIND

> "List to the whoop and whistle of the winds,
> Their hollow drone as they come roaring on,
> For strength hath many a voice, and when aroused
> The flying tempest calls with awful joy
> And echoes as it strikes the mountain-side,
> Then crashes in the forest. Hear the cry!
> Surely a god hath set his lions loose
> And laughs to hear them as they rage afar."
>
> —C. G. LELAND.

THE following story does not belong to the Gospel of the Witches, but I add it as it confirms the fact that the worship of *Diana* existed for a long time contemporary with Christianity. Its full title in the orginal MS., which was written out by Maddalena, after hearing it from a man who was a native of Volterra, is *La Pellegrina della Casa al Vento*—"The Female Pilgrim of the House of the Wind." It may be added that, as the tale declares, the house in question is still standing.

There is a peasant's house at the beginning of the hill or ascent leading to Volterra, and it is called the House of the Wind. Near it there once stood a small palace, wherein dwelt a married couple, who had but one child, a daughter, whom they adored. Truly if the child had but a headache, they each had a worse attack from fear.

Little by little the girl grew older, and all the thought of the mother, who was very devout, was that she should become a nun. But the girl did not like this, and declared that she hoped to be married like others. And when looking from her window one day, she saw and heard the birds singing in the vines and among the trees all so merrily, she said to her mother that she hoped some day to have a family of little birds of her own, singing round her in a cheerful nest. At which the mother was so angry that she gave her daughter a cuff. And the young lady wept, but replied with spirit, that if beaten or treated in any such manner, that she would certainly soon find some way to escape and get married, for she had no idea of being made a nun of against her will.

At hearing this the mother was seriously frightened, for she knew the spirit of her child, and was afraid lest the girl already had a lover, and would make a great scandal over the blow; and turning it all over, she thought of an elderly lady of good family, but much reduced, who was famous for her intelligence, learning, and power of persuasion, and she thought, "This will be just the person to induce my daughter to become pious, and fill her head with devotion and make a nun of her." So she sent for this clever person, who was at once appointed the governess and constant attendant of the young lady, who, instead of quarrelling with her guardian, became devoted to her.

However, everything in this world does not go exactly as we would have it, and no one knows what fish or crab may hide under a rock in a river. For it so happened that the governess was not a Catholic at all, as will presently appear, and did not vex her pupil with any threats of a nun's life, nor even with an approval of it.

It came to pass that the young lady, who was in the habit of lying awake on moonlight nights to hear the nightingales sing, thought she heard her governess in the next room, of which the door was open, rise and go forth on the great balcony. The next night the same thing took place, and rising very softly and unseen, she beheld the lady praying, or at least kneeling in the moonlight, which seemed to her to be very singular conduct, the more so because the lady kneeling uttered words which the younger could not understand, and which certainly formed no part of the Church service.

And being much exercised over the strange occurrence, she at last, with timid excuses, told her governess what she had seen. Then the latter, after a little reflection, first binding her to a secrecy of life and death, for, as she declared, it was a matter of great peril, spoke as follows :—

"I, like thee, was instructed when young by priests to worship an invisible god. But an old woman in whom I had great confidence once said to me, 'Why worship a deity whom you cannot see, when there is the Moon in all her splendour visible? Worship her. Invoke *Diana*, the goddess of the Moon, and she will grant your prayers.' This shalt thou do, obeying the *Vangelo*, the Gospel of (the Witches and of) *Diana*, who is Queen of the Fairies and of the Moon."

Now the young lady being persuaded, was converted to the worship of *Diana* and the Moon, and having prayed with all her heart for a lover (having learned the conjuration to the goddess),[1] was soon rewarded by the attention and devotion of a brave and wealthy cavalier, who was indeed as admirable a suitor as any one could desire. But the mother, who was far more bent on gratifying vindictiveness and cruel vanity than on her daughter's happiness, was infuriated at this, and when the gentleman came to her, she bade him begone, for her daughter was vowed to become a nun, and a nun she should be or die.

Then the young lady was shut up in a cell in a tower, without even the company of her governess, and put to strong and hard pain, being made to sleep on the stone floor, and would have 'died of hunger had her mother had her way.

Then in this dire need she prayed to *Diana* to set her free; when lo! she found the prison door unfastened, and easily escaped. Then having obtained a pilgrim's dress, she travelled far and wide, teaching and preaching the religion of old times, the religion of *Diana*, the Queen of the Fairies and of the Moon, the goddess of the poor and the oppressed.

And the fame of her wisdom and beauty went forth over all the land, and people worshipped her, calling her *La Bella Pellegrina*. At last her mother, hearing of her,

[1] This incantation is given in the chapter entitled "A Spell to Win Love."

was in a greater rage than ever, and, in fine, after much trouble, succeeded in having her again arrested and cast into prison. And then in evil temper indeed she asked her whether she would become a nun; to which she replied that it was not possible, because she had left the Catholic Church and become a worshipper of *Diana* and of the Moon.

And the end of it was that the mother, regarding her daughter as lost, gave her up to the priests to be put to torture and death, as they did all who would not agree with them or who left their religion.

But the people were not well pleased with this, because they adored her beauty and goodness, and there were few who had not enjoyed her charity.

But by the aid of her lover she obtained, as a last grace, that on the night before she was to be tortured and executed she might, with a guard, go forth into the garden of the palace and pray.

This she did, and standing by the door of the house, which is still there, prayed in the light of the full moon to *Diana*, that she might be delivered from the dire persecution to which she had been subjected, since even her own parents had willingly given her over to an awful death.

Now her parents and the priests, and all who sought her death, were in the palace watching lest she should escape.

When lo! in answer to her prayer there came a terrible tempest and overwhelming wind, a storm such as man had never seen before, which overthrew and swept away the palace with all who were in it; there was not one stone left upon another, nor one soul alive of all who were there. The gods had replied to the prayer.

The young lady escaped happily with her lover, wedded him, and the house of the peasant where the lady stood is still called *La Casa al Vento*, or the House of the Wind.

This is very accurately the *story* as I received it, but I freely admit that I have very much condensed the language of the original text, which consists of twenty pages, and which, as regards needless padding, indicates a capacity on the part of the narrator to write an average modern fashionable novel, even a second-rate French one, which is saying a great deal. It is true that there are in it no detailed descriptions of scenery, skies, trees, or clouds—and a great deal might be made of Volterra in that way—but it is prolonged in a manner which shows a gift for it. However, the narrative itself is strangely original and vigorous, for it is such a relic of pure classic heathenism, and such a survival of faith in the old mythology, as all the reflected second-hand Hellenism of the Æsthetes cannot equal. That a real worship of or belief in classic divinities should have survived to the present day in the very land of Papacy itself, is a much more curious fact than if a living mammoth had been discovered in some out of the way corner of the earth, because the former is a human phenomenon. I foresee that the day will come, and that perhaps not so very far distant, when the world of scholars will be amazed to consider to what a late period an immense body of antique tradition survived in Northern Italy, and how indifferent the learned were regarding it; there having been in very truth only one man, and he a foreigner, who earnestly occupied himself with collecting and preserving it.

It is very probable that there were as many touching episodes among the heathen martyrs who were forced to give up their beloved deities, such as Diana, Venus, the Graces, and others, who were worshipped for beauty, as there were even among the Christians who were thrown to the lions. For the heathen *loved* their gods with a human personal sympathy, without mysticism or fear, as if they had been blood-relations; and there were many among them who really believed that such was the case when some damsel who had made a *faux pas* got out of it by attributing it all to some god, faun, or satyr; which is very touching. There is a great deal to be said for as well as against the idolaters or worshippers of dolls, as I heard a small girl define them.

CHAPTER XII

TANA, THE MOON-GODDESS

THE following story, which appeared originally in the *Legends of Florence*, collected from the people by me, does not properly belong to the Witch's Gospel, as it is not strictly in accordance with it; and yet it could not well be omitted, since it is on the same subject. In it *Diana* appears simply as the lunar goddess of chastity, therefore not as a witch. It was given to me as *Fana*, but my informant said that it might be *Tana*; she was not sure. As *Tana* occurs in another tale, and as the subject is certainly *Diana*, there can hardly be a question of this.

Tana, la Dea della Luna.

Tana was a very beautiful girl, but extremely poor, and as modest and pure as she was beautiful and humble. She went from one contadino to another, or from farm to farm to work, and thus led an honest life.

There was a young boor, a very ugly, bestial, and brutish fellow, who was after his fashion raging with love for her, but she could not so much as bear to look at him, and repelled all his advances.

But late one night, when she was returning alone from the farmhouse where she had worked to her home, this man, who had hidden himself in a thicket, leaped out on her and cried, "*Non mi sfuggerai; sara mia!*"—"Thou canst not flee; mine thou shalt be!"

And seeing no help near, and only the full moon looking down on her from heaven, Tana in despair cast herself on her knees and cried to it:—

"I have no one on earth to defend me,
Thou alone dost see me in this strait;
Therefore I pray to thee, O Moon!
As thou art beautiful so thou art bright,
Flashing thy splendour over all mankind;
Even so I pray thee light up the mind
Of this poor ruffian, who would wrong me here,
Even to the worst. Cast light into his soul,
That he may let me be in peace, and then
Return in all thy light unto my home!"

When she had said this, there appeared before her a bright but shadowy form—*una ombra bianca*—which said:—

"Rise, and go to thy home!
Thou hast well deserved this grace;
No one shall trouble thee more,
Purest of all on earth!
Thou shalt a goddess be,
The Goddess of the Moon,
Of all enchantment queen!"

Thus it came to pass that *Tana* became the *dea* or spirit of the Moon.

Though the air be set to a different key, this is a poem of pure melody, and the same as Wordsworth's "Goody Blake and Harry Gill." Both *Tana* and the old dame are surprised and terrified ; both pray to a power above :—

> "The cold, cold moon above her head,
> Thus on her knees did Goody pray ;
> Young Harry heard what she had said,
> And icy cold he turned away."

The dramatic centre is just the same in both. The English ballad soberly turns into an incurable fit of ague inflicted on a greedy young boor ; the Italian witch-poetess, with finer sense, or with more sympathy for the heroine, casts the brute aside without further mention, and apotheosises the maiden, identifying her with the Moon. The former is more practical and probable, the latter more *poetical.*

And here it is worth while, despite digression, to remark what an immense majority there are of people who can perceive, feel, and value poetry in mere words or *form*—that is to say, objectively—and hardly know or note it when it is presented subjectively or as thought, but not put into some kind of verse or measure, or regulated form. This is a curious experiment and worth studying. Take a passage from some famous poet ; write it out in pure simple prose, doing full justice to its real meaning, and if it still actually thrills or moves as poetry, then it is of the first class. But if it has lost its glamour absolutely, it is *second-rate* or inferior; for the best cannot be made out of mere words varnished with associations, be they of thought or feeling.

This is not such a far cry from the subject as might be deemed. Reading and feeling them subjectively, I am often struck by the fact that in these Witch traditions which I have gathered there is a wondrous poetry of thought, which far excels the efforts of many modern bards, and which only requires the aid of some clever workman in words to assume the highest rank. A proof of what I have asserted may be found in the fact that, in such famous poems as the *Finding of the Lyre*, by James Russell Lowell, and that on the invention of the pipe by Pan, by Mrs. Browning, that which formed the most exquisite and refined portion of the original myths is omitted by both authors, simply because they missed or did not perceive it. For in the former we are not told that it was the breathing of the god *Air* (who was the inspiring soul of ancient music, and the *Bellaria* of modern witch-mythology) on the dried filament of the tortoise, which suggested to Hermes the making an instrument wherewith he made the music of the spheres and guided the course of the planets. As for Mrs.

Browning, she leaves out *Syrinx* altogether, that is to say, the voice of the nymph still lingering in the pipe which had been her body. Now to my mind the old prose narrative of these myths is much more deeply poetical and moving, and far more inspired with beauty and romance, than are the well-rhymed and measured, but very imperfect versions given by our poets. And in fact, such want of intelligence or perception may be found in all the "classic" poems, not only of Keats, but of almost every poet of the age who has dealt in Greek subjects.

Great license is allowed to painters and poets, but when they take a subject, especially a deep tradition, and fail to perceive its *real meaning* or catch its point, and simply give us something very pretty, but not so inspired with meaning as the original, it can hardly be claimed that they have done their work as it might, or, in fact, should have been done. I find that this fault does not occur in the Italian or Tuscan witch-versions of the ancient fables; on the contrary, they keenly appreciate, and even expand, the antique spirit. Hence I have often had occasion to remark that it was not impossible that in some cases popular tradition, even as it now exists, has been preserved more fully and accurately than we find it in any Latin writer.

Now apropos of missing the point, I would

remind certain very literal readers that if they find many faults of grammar, mis-spelling, and worse in the Italian texts in this book, they will not, as a distinguished reviewer has done, attribute them all to the ignorance of the author, but to the imperfect education of the person who collected and recorded them. I am reminded of this by having seen in a circulating library a copy of my *Legends of Florence*, in which some good careful soul had taken pains with a pencil to correct all the archaisms. Wherein he or she was like a certain Boston proof-reader, who in a book of mine changed the spelling of many citations from Chaucer, Spenser, and others into the purest, or impurest, Webster; he being under the impression that I was extremely ignorant of orthography. As for the writing in or injuring books, which always belong partly to posterity, it is a sin of vulgarity as well as morality, and indicates *what people are* more than they dream.

> "Only a cad as low as a thief
> Would write in a book or turn down a leaf,
> Since 'tis thievery, as well is known,
> To make free with that which is not our own."

CHAPTER XIII

DIANA AND THE CHILDREN

"And there withall Diana gan appere
With bowe in hand right as an Hunteresse,
And saydê, 'Daughter, stint thine heavinesse!'
And forth she wente and made a vanishing."
—CHAUCER (*C. T.*), "*The Knight's Tale.*"

THERE was in Florence in the oldest time a noble family, but grown so poor that their *giorni di festa* or feast-days were few and far between. However, they dwelt in their old palace (which was in the street now called La Via Cittadella), which was a fine old building, and so they kept up a brave show before the world, when many a day they hardly had anything to eat.

Round this palace was a large garden, in which stood an ancient marble statue of *Diana*, like a beautiful woman who seemed to be running with a dog by her side. She held in her hand a bow, and on her forehead was a small moon. And it was said that by night, when all was still, the statue became like life and fled, and did not return till the moon set or the sun rose.

The father of the family had two children, who were good and intelligent. One day they came home with many flowers which had been given to them, and the little girl said to her brother:—

"The beautiful lady with the bow ought to have some of these!"

Saying this, they laid flowers before the statue and made a wreath which the boy placed on her head.

Just then the great poet and magician Virgil, who knew everything about the gods and fairies, entered the garden and said, smiling:—

"You have made the offering of flowers to the goddess quite correctly, as they did of old; all that remains is to pronounce the prayer properly,[1] and it is this:"

So he repeated the

Invocation to Diana.

Bella dea dell' arco!
Bella dea delle freccie!
Della caccia e dei cani!
Tu vegli colle stelle,
Quando il sole va dormir
Tu colla luna in fronte
Cacci la notte meglio del di.
Colle tue Ninfe al suono
Di trombe—Sei la regina
Dei cacciatori—regina della notte,
Tu che sei la cacciatrice
Più potenti di ogni,
Cacciator—ti prego
Pensa un poco a noi!

1 The most important part of witchcraft is to *intone* or accent the incantations accurately, in a manner like that of church chanting or Arab recitations. Hence the apparently prose form of most spells.

To Diana.

Lovely Goddess of the bow!
Lovely Goddess of the arrows!
Of all hounds and of all hunting
Thou who wakest in starry heaven
When the sun is sunk in slumber
Thou with moon upon thy forehead,
Who the chase by night preferrest
Unto hunting in the daylight,
With thy nymphs unto the music
Of the horn—thyself the huntress,
And most powerful: I pray thee
Think, although but for an instant,
Upon us who pray unto thee![1]

Then Virgil taught them also the *Scongiurazione* or spell to be uttered when good fortune or aught is specially required.

The Conjuration to Diana.

"Bella dea del arco del cielo!
Delle stelle e della luna!
La regina più potente
Dei cacciatori e della notte!
A te ricorriamo,
E chiedamo il tuo aiuto
Che tu possa darci
Sempre la buona fortuna!"

[1] It is to be observed that the invocation is strictly a psalm of praise or a hymn; the *scongiurazione* is a request or prayer, though it often takes the form of a threat or menace. This only exists in classic witchcraft.

Fair goddess of the rainbow,
Of the stars and of the moon!
The queen most powerful
Of hunters and the night!
We beg of thee thy aid,
That thou may'st give to us
The best of fortune ever!

Then he added the conclusion:—

"Se la nostra scongiurazione
Ascolterai,
E buona fortuna ci darei,
Un segnale a noi lo darei!"

If thou heed'st our evocation
And wilt give good fortune to us,
Then in proof give us a token![1]

[1] Something is here omitted, which can, however, be supplied from many other similar incantations. It was probably as follows:—

If thou art favourable
And wilt grant my prayer,
Then may I hear
The bark of a dog,
The neigh of a horse,
The croaking of a frog,
The chirp of a bird,
The song of a cricket,
et cætera.

Three or four of these sounds were generally selected. They vary more or less, but seldom materially, from these. Sometimes visible manifestations, as, for instance, lightning, are requested. To see a white horse is a sign that the prayer will be granted after some delay. It also signifies *victory*.

F

And having taught them this, Virgil departed.

Then the children ran to tell their parents all that had happened, and the latter impressed it on them to keep it a secret, nor breathe a word or hint thereof to any one. But what was their amazement when they found early the next morning before the statue a deer freshly killed, which gave them good dinners for many a day; nor did they want thereafter at any time game of all kinds, when the prayer had been devoutly pronounced.

There was a neighbour of this family, a priest, who held in hate all the ways and worship of the gods of the old time, and whatever did not belong to *his* religion, and he, passing the garden one day, beheld the statue of *Diana* crowned with roses and (other) flowers. And being in a rage, and seeing in the street a decayed cabbage, he rolled it in the mud, and threw it all dripping at the face of the goddess, saying:—

"Ecco mala bestia d' idoli!
Questo e l' omaggio che io ti do,
Gia che il diavolo ti aiuta!"

Behold, thou vile beast of idolatry,
This is the worship which thou hast from me,
And the devil do the rest for thee!

Then the priest heard a voice in the gloom where the leaves were dense, and it said:—

"Bene, bene! Tu mi hai fatto
L' offrando—tu avrai
La tua porzione
Della mia caccia. Aspetta!"

It is well! I give thee warning,
Since thou hast made thy offering,
Some of the game to thee I'll bring;
Thou'lt have thy share in the morning.

All that night the priest suffered from horrible dreams and dread, and when at last, just before three o'clock, he fell asleep, he suddenly awoke from a nightmare in which it seemed as if something heavy rested on his chest. And something indeed fell from him and rolled on the floor. And when he rose and picked it up, and looked at it by the light of the moon, he saw that it was a human head, half decayed.[1]

Another priest, who had heard his cry of terror, entered his room, and having looked at the head, said:—

"I know that face! It is of a man whom I confessed, and who was beheaded three months ago at Siena."

And three days after the priest who had insulted the goddess died.

The foregoing tale was not given to me as belonging to the Gospel of the Witches, but as one of a very large series of traditions relating to *Virgil* as a magician. But it has its proper place in this book, because it contains the invocation to and incantation of *Diana*, these being remarkably beautiful and original. When we

1 "La testa d' un uomo piena di verme e puzzolente." A parody in kind for the decayed cabbage, much completer than the end of the German tale resembling it.

remember how these "hymns" have been handed down or preserved by old women, and doubtless much garbled, changed, and deformed by transmission, it cannot but seem wonderful that so much classic beauty still remains in them, as, for instance, in

"Lovely goddess of the bow!
Lovely goddess of the arrow!
Thou who walk'st in starry heaven!"

Robert Browning was a great poet, but if we compare all the Italian witch-poems of and to *Diana* with the former's much-admired speech of Diana-Artemis, it will certainly be admitted by impartial critics that the spells are fully equal to the following by the bard—

"I am a goddess of the ambrosial courts,
And save by Here, Queen of Pride, surpassed
By none whose temples whiten this the world:
Through Heaven I roll my lucid moon along,
I shed in Hell o'er my pale people peace,
On Earth, I, caring for the creatures, guard
Each pregnant yellow wolf and fox-bitch sleek,
And every feathered mother's callow brood,
And all that love green haunts and loneliness."

This is pretty, but it is only imitation, and neither in form or spirit really equal to the incantations, which are sincere in faith. And it may here be observed in sorrow, yet in very truth, that in a very great number of modern poetical handlings of classic mythic subjects, the writers have, despite all their genius as artists, produced rococo work which will appear to be such to another generation, simply from their having missed the point, or omitted from ignorance something vital which the folk-lorist would probably not have lost. *Achilles* may be admirably drawn, as I have seen him, in a Louis XIV. wig with a Turkish scimitar, but still one could wish that the designer had been a little more familiar with Greek garments and weapons.

CHAPTER XIV

THE GOBLIN MESSENGERS OF DIANA AND MERCURY

THE following tale was not given to me as connected with the Gospel of the Witches, but as *Diana* appears in it, and as the whole conception is that of *Diana* and *Apollo* in another form, I include it in the series.

Many centuries ago there was a *folletto*, goblin, or spirit, or devil-angel—*chi sa?*—who knows what?—and *Mercurio*, who was the god of speed and of quickness, being much pleased with this imp, bestowed on him the gift of running like the wind, with the privilege that whatever he pursued, be it spirit, a human being, or animal, he should certainly overtake or catch it.

This *folletto* had a beautiful sister, who, like him, ran errands, not for the gods, but for the goddesses (there was a female god for every male, even down to the small spirits); and *Diana* on the same day gave to this fairy the power that, whoever might chase her, she should, if pursued, never be overtaken.

One day the brother saw his sister speeding like a flash of lightning across the heaven, and he felt a sudden strange desire in rivalry to overtake her. So he dashed after as she flitted on; but though it was his destiny to catch, she had been fated never to be caught, and so the will of one supreme god was balanced by that of another.

So the two kept flying round and round the edge of heaven, and at first all the gods roared with laughter, but when they understood the case, they grew serious, and asked one another how it was to end.

Then the great father-god said:—

"Behold the earth, which is in darkness and gloom! I will change the sister into a moon, and her brother into a sun. And so shall she ever escape him, yet will he ever catch her with his light, which shall fall on her from afar; for the rays of the sun are his hands, which reach forth with burning grasp, yet which are ever eluded."

And thus it is said that this race begins anew with the first of every month, when the moon being cold, *is covered with as many coats as an onion.* But while the race is being run, as the moon becomes warm she casts off one garment after another, till she is naked and then stops, and then when dressed the race begins again.

As the vast storm-cloud falls in glittering drops, even so the great myths of the olden time are broken up into small fairy-tales, and as these drops in turn reunite

"En rivière ou sur l'estang,"

("On silent lake or streamlet lone,")

as Villon hath it, even so minor myths are again formed from the fallen waters. In this story we clearly have the dog made by Vulcan and the wolf—Jupiter settled the question by petrifying them—as you may read in *Julius Pollux* his fifth book, or any other on mythology. *Is canis fuit postea à Jove in lapidem conversus.*

> "Which hunting hound, as well is known,
> Was changed by Jupiter to stone."

It is remarkable that in this story the moon is compared to an onion. "The onion," says Friedrich (*Symbolik der Natur*, p. 348), "was, on account of its many skins, among the Egyptians the emblem and hieroglyph of the many-formed moon, whose different phases are so clearly seen in the root when it is cut through, also because its growth or decrease corresponds with that of the planet. Therefore it was dedicated to Isis, the Moon-Goddess." And for this reason the onion was so holy as to be regarded as having in itself something of deity; for which reason Juvenal remarks that the Egyptians were happy people to have gods growing in their gardens.

CHAPTER XV

LAVERNA

THE following very curious tale, with the incantation, was not in the text of the *Vangelo*, but it very evidently belongs to the cycle or series of legends connected with it. *Diana* is declared to be the protectress of all outcasts, those to whom the night is their day, consequently of thieves; and *Laverna*, as we may learn from *Horace* (*Epistles*, 16, 1) and *Plautus*, was pre-eminently the patroness of pilfering and all rascality. In this story she also appears as a witch and humourist.

It was given to me as a tradition of *Virgil*, who often appears as one familiar with the marvellous and hidden lore of the olden time.

It happened on a time that Virgil, who knew all things hidden or magical, he who was a magician and poet, having heard a speech (or oration) by a famous talker who had not much in him, was asked what he thought of it? And he replied:—

"It seems to me to be impossible to tell whether it was all introduction or all conclusion; certainly there was no body in it. It was like certain fish of whom one is in doubt whether they are all head or all tail, or only head and tail; or the goddess Laverna, of whom no one ever knew whether she was all head or all body, or neither or both."

Then the emperor inquired who this deity might be, for he had never heard of her.

And Virgil replied:—

"Among the gods or spirits who were of ancient times—may they be ever favourable to us! Among them (was) one female who was the craftiest and most knavish of them all. She was called *Laverna.* She was a thief, and very little known to the other deities, who were honest and dignified, for she was rarely in heaven or in the country of the fairies.

"She was almost always on earth, among thieves, pickpockets, and panders—she lived in darkness.

"Once it happened that she went (to a mortal), a great priest in the form and guise of a very beautiful stately priestess (of some goddess), and said to him:—

"'You have an estate which I wish to buy. I intend to build on it a temple to (our) God. I swear to you on my body that I will pay thee within a year.'

"Therefore the priest transferred to her the estate.

"And very soon *Laverna* had sold off all the crops, grain, cattle, wood, and poultry. There was not left the value of four farthings.

"But on the day fixed for payment there was no

Laverna to be seen. The fair goddess was far away, and had left her creditor *in asso*—in the lurch!

"At the same time *Laverna* went to a great lord and bought of him a castle, well-furnished within and broad rich lands without.

"But this time she swore on her *head* to pay in full in six months.

"And as she had done by the priest, so she acted to the lord of the castle, and stole and sold every stick, furniture, cattle, men, and mice—there was not left wherewith to feed a fly.

"Then the priest and the lord, finding out who this was, appealed to the gods, complaining that they had been robbed by a goddess.

"And it was soon made known to them all that this was *Laverna.*

"Therefore she was called to judgment before all the gods.

"And when she was asked what she had done with the property of the priest, unto whom she had sworn by her body to make payment at the time appointed (and why had she broken her oath)?

"She replied by a strange deed which amazed them all, for she made her body disappear, so that only her head remained visible, and it cried:—

"'Behold me! I swore by my body, but body have I none!'

"Then all the gods laughed.

"After the priest came the lord who had also been tricked, and to whom she had sworn by her head. And in reply to him *Laverna* showed to all present her whole body without mincing matters, and it was one of extreme beauty, but without a head; and from the neck thereof came a voice which said:—

'Behold me, for I am *Laverna*, who
Have come to answer to that lord's complaint,
Who swears that I contracted debt to him,
And have not paid although the time is o'er,
And that I am a thief because I swore
Upon my *head*—but, as you all can see,
I have no head at all, and therefore I
Assuredly ne'er swore by such an oath.'

"Then there was indeed a storm of laughter among the gods, who made the matter right by ordering the head to join the body, and bidding *Laverna* pay up her debts, which she did.

"Then *Jove* spoke and said:—

"'Here is a roguish goddess without a duty (or a worshipper), while there are in Rome innumerable thieves, sharpers, cheats, and rascals—*ladri, bindolini, truffatori e scrocconi*—who live by deceit.

"'These good folk have neither a church nor a god, and it is a great pity, for even the very devils have their master, Satan, as the head of the family. Therefore, I command that in future *Laverna* shall be the goddess of all the knaves or dishonest tradesmen, with the whole rubbish and refuse of the human race, who have been hitherto without a god or a devil, inasmuch as they have been too despicable for the one or the other.'

"And so *Laverna* became the goddess of all dishonest and shabby people.

"Whenever any one planned or intended any knavery or aught wicked, he entered her temple, and invoked *Laverna*, who appeared to him as a woman's head. But if he did his work of knavery badly or maladroitly, when he again invoked her he saw only the body; but if he was clever, then he beheld the whole goddess, head and body.

"*Laverna* was no more chaste than she was honest, and had many lovers and many children. It was said that not being bad at heart or cruel, she often repented her life and sins; but do what she might, she could not reform, because her passions were so inveterate.

"And if a man had got any woman with child or any maid found herself *enceinte*, and would hide it from the world and escape scandal, they would go[1] every day to invoke *Laverna*.

"Then when the time came for the suppliant to be delivered, *Laverna* would bear her in sleep during the night to her temple, and after the birth cast her into slumber again, and bear her back to her bed at home. And when she awoke in the morning, she was ever in vigorous health and felt no weariness, and all seemed to her as a dream.[2]

"But to those who desired in time to reclaim their

[1] This was a very peculiar characteristic of *Diana*, who was involved in a similar manner. I have here omitted much needless verbiage or repetition in the original MS. and also abbreviated what follows.

[2] All of this indicates unmistakably, in several respects, a genuine tradition. In the hands of crafty priests this would prove a great aid to popularity.

children, *Laverna* was indulgent if they led such lives as pleased her and faithfully worshipped her.

"And this is the ceremony to be performed and the incantation to be offered every night to *Laverna*.

"There must be a set place devoted to the goddess, be it a room, a cellar, or a grove, but ever a solitary place.

"Then take a small table of the size of forty playing-cards set close together, and this must be hid in the same place, and going there at night . . .

"Take forty cards and spread them on the table, making of them a close carpet or cover on it.

"Take of the herbs *paura* and *concordia*, and boil the two together, repeating meanwhile the following:—

Scongiurazione.

Fa bollire la mano della concordia,
Per tenere a me concordo,
La Laverna che possa portare a me
Il mio figlio, e che possa
Guardarmele da qualun pericolo.

Bollo questa erba, man non bollo l' erba.
Bollo la *paura* [1] che possa tenere lontano
Qualunque persona e se le viene
L' idea a qualchuno di avvicinarsi,
Possa essere preso da *paura*
E fuggire lontano!

[1] I conjecture that this is wild poppy. The poppy was specially sacred to Ceres, but also to the Night and its rites, and *Laverna* was a nocturnal deity—a play on the word *paura*, or fear.

Incantation.

I boil the cluster of concordia
To keep in concord and at peace with me
Laverna, that she may restore to me
My child, and that she by her favouring care
May guard me well from danger all my life!
I boil this herb, yet 'tis not it which boils;
I boil the *fear*, that it may keep afar
Any intruder, and if such should come
(To spy upon my rite), may he be struck
With fear and in his terror haste away![1]

Having said thus, put the boiled herbs in a bottle and spread the cards on the table one by one, saying:—

Batezzo queste quaranta carte!
Ma non batezzo le quaranta carte,
Battezzo quaranta dei superi,
Alla dea *Laverna* che le sue
Persone divengono un Vulcano
Fino che la *Laverna* non sara
Venuta da me colla mia creatura,
E questi dei dal naso dalla bocca,
E dal' orecchio possino buttare
Fiammi di fuoco e cenere,

[1] This passage recalls strangely enough the worship of the Græco-Roman goddess *Pavor* or Fear, the attendant on Mars. She was much invoked, as in the present instance, to terrify intruders or an enemy. *Æschylus* makes the seven chiefs before Thebes swear by *Fear*, Mars, and Bellona. *Mem. Acad. of Inscriptions*, v. 9.

E lasciare pace e bene alla dea
Laverna, che possa anche essa
Abbraciare i suoi fighi
A sua volunta !

Incantation.

I spread before me now the forty cards,
Yet 'tis not forty cards which here I spread,
But forty of the gods superior
To the deity *Laverna*, that their forms
May each and all become volcanoes hot,
Until *Laverna* comes and brings my child ;
And 'till 'tis done may they all cast at her
Hot flames of fire, and with them glowing coals
From noses, mouths, and ears (until she yields) ;
Then may they leave *Laverna* to her peace,
Free to embrace her children at her will !

"*Laverna* was the Roman goddess of thieves, pickpockets, shopkeepers or dealers, plagiarists, rascals, and hypocrites. There was near Rome a temple in a grove where robbers went to divide their plunder. There was a statue of the goddess. Her image, according to some, was a head without a body ; according to others, a body without a head ; but the epithet of 'beautiful' applied to her by Horace indicates that she who gave disguises to her worshippers had kept one to herself." She was worshipped in perfect silence.

This is confirmed by a passage in Horace (*Epist.* 16, lib. 1), where an impostor, hardly daring to move his lips, repeats the following prayer or incantation :—

"O Goddess *Laverna!*
Give me the art of cheating and deceiving,
Of making men believe that I am just,
Holy, and innocent! extend all darkness
And deep obscurity o'er my misdeeds!"

It is interesting to compare this unquestionably ancient classic invocation to *Laverna* with the one which is before given. The goddess was extensively known to the lower orders, and in Plautus a cook who has been robbed of his implements calls on her to revenge him.

I call special attention to the fact that in this, as in a great number of Italian witch-incantations, the deity or spirit who is worshipped, be it *Diana* herself or *Laverna,* is *threatened* with torment by a higher power until he or she grants the favour demanded. This is quite classic, *i.e.,* Græco-Roman or Oriental, in all of which sources the magician relies not on favour, aid, or power granted by either God or Satan, but simply on what he has been able to wrench and wring, as it were, out of infinite nature or the primal source by penance and study. I mention this because a reviewer has reproached me with exaggerating the degree to which *diabolism*—introduced by the Church since 1500—is deficient in Italy. But in fact, among the higher class of witches, or in their traditions, it is hardly to be found at all. In Christian diabolism the witch never dares to threaten Satan or God, or any of the Trinity or angels, for the whole system is based on the conception of a Church and of obedience.

The herb concordia probably takes its name from that of the goddess Concordia, who was represented as holding a branch. It plays a great part in witchcraft, after verbena and rue.

APPENDIX

APPENDIX

COMMENTS ON THE FOREGOING TEXTS

So long ago as the year 1886 I learned that there was in existence a manuscript setting forth the doctrines of Italian witchcraft, and I was promised that, if possible, it should be obtained for me. In this I was for a time disappointed. But having urged it on MADDALENA, my collector of folk-lore, while she was leading a wandering life in Tuscany, to make an effort to obtain or recover something of the kind, I at last received from her, on January 1, 1897, from Colle, Val d'Elsa, near Siena, the MS. entitled *Aradia, or the Gospel of the Witches.*

Now be it observed, that every leading point which forms the plot or centre of this *Vangel*, such as that *Diana* is Queen of the Witches; an associate of *Herodias* (*Aradia*) in her relations to sorcery; that she bore a child to her brother the Sun (here *Lucifer*); that as a moon-goddess she is in some relation to Cain, who dwells as prisoner in the moon, and that the witches of old were people oppressed by feudal lands, the former revenging themselves in every way, and holding orgies to *Diana* which the Church represented as being the worship of Satan—all of this, I repeat, had been told or written out for me in fragments by Maddalena (not to speak of other authorities), even as it had been chronicled by Horst or Michelet; therefore all this is in the present document of minor importance. All of this I expected, but what I did not expect, and what was new to me, was that portion which is given as prose-poetry and which I have *rendered* in metre or verse. This being traditional, and taken down from wizards, is extremely curious and interesting, since in it are preserved many relics of lore which, as may be verified from records, have come down from days of yore.

Aradia is evidently enough *Herodias*, who was regarded in the beginning as associated with *Diana* as chief of the witches. This was not, as I opine, derived from the *Herodias* of the New Testament, but from an earlier replica of *Lilith*, bearing the same name. It is, in fact, an identification or twin-ing of the Aryan and Shemitic Queens of Heaven, or of Night and of Sorcery, and it may be that this was known to the earliest myth-makers. So far back as the sixth century the worship of *Herodias* and *Diana* by witches was condemned by a Church Council at Ancyra. Pipernus and other writers have noted the evident identity of *Herodias* with *Lilith*. *Isis* preceded both.

Diana is very vigorously, even dramatically, set forth in this poem as the goddess of the god-forsaken and ungodly, of thieves, harlots, and, truthfully enough, of the "minions of the moon," as Falstaff would have fain had them called. It was recognised in ancient Rome, as it is in modern India, that no human being *can* be so bad or vile as to have forfeited all right to divine protection of some kind or other, and *Diana* was this protectress. It may be as well to observe here, that among all free-thinking philosophers, educated *parias*, and literary or book-Bohemians, there has ever been a most unorthodox tendency to believe that the faults and errors of humanity are more due (if not altogether due) to unavoidable causes which we cannot help, as, for instance, heredity, the being born savages, or poor, or in vice, or unto "bigotry and virtue" in excess, or unto inquisitioning—that is to say, when we are so overburdened with innately born sin that all our free will cannot set us free from it.[1]

It was during the so-called Dark Ages, or from the downfall of the Roman Empire until the thirteenth century, that the belief that all

[1] Hence the saying that to know all would be to forgive all; which may be nine-tenths true, but there *is* a tenth of responsible guilt.

which was worst in man owed its origin solely to the monstrous abuses and tyranny of Church and State. For then, at every turn in life, the vast majority encountered downright shameless, palpable iniquity and injustice, with no law for the weak who were without patrons.

The perception of this drove vast numbers of the discontented into rebellion, and as they could not prevail by open warfare, they took their hatred out in a form of secret anarchy, which was, however, intimately blended with superstition and fragments of old tradition. Prominent in this, and naturally enough, was the worship of *Diana* the protectress—for the alleged adoration of Satan was a far later invention of the Church, and it has never really found a leading place in Italian witchcraft to this day. That is to say, purely *diabolical* witchcraft did not find general acceptance till the end of the fifteenth century, when it was, one may almost say, invented in Rome to supply means wherewith to destroy the threatening heresy of Germany.

The growth of Sentiment is the increase of suffering; man is never entirely miserable until he finds out how wronged he is and fancies that he sees far ahead a possible freedom. In ancient times men as slaves suffered less under even more abuse, because they believed they were born to low conditions of life. Even the best reform brings pain with it, and the great awakening of man was accompanied with griefs, many of which even yet endure. Pessimism is the result of too much culture and *introversion.*

It appears to be strangely out of sight and out of mind with all historians, that the sufferings of the vast majority of mankind, or the enslaved and poor, were far greater under early Christianity, or till the end of the Middle Ages and the Emancipation of Serfs, than they were before. The reason for this was that in the old "heathen" time the humble did not know, or even dream, that all are equal before God, or that they had many *rights*, even here on earth, as slaves; for, in fact, the whole *moral* tendency of the New Testament is utterly opposed to slavery, or even severe servitude. Every word uttered teaching Christ's mercy and love, humility and charity, was, in fact, a bitter reproof, not only to every lord in the land, but to the Church itself, and its arrogant prelates. The fact that many abuses had been mitigated and that there were benevolent saints, does not affect the fact that, on the whole, mankind was for a long time worse off than before, and the greatest cause of this suffering was what may be called a sentimental one, or a newly-born consciousness of rights withheld, which is always of itself a torture. And this was greatly aggravated by the endless preaching to the people that it was a *duty* to suffer and endure oppression and tyranny, and that the rights of Authority of all kinds were so great that they on the whole even excused their worst abuses. For by upholding Authority in the nobility the Church maintained its own.

The result of it all was a vast development of rebels, outcasts, and all the discontented, who adopted witchcraft or sorcery for a religion, and wizards as their priests. They had secret meetings in desert places, among old ruins accursed by priests as the haunt of evil spirits or ancient heathen gods, or in the mountains. To this day the dweller in Italy may often find secluded spots environed by ancient chestnut forests, rocks, and walls, which suggest fit places for the *Sabbat*, and are sometimes still believed by tradition to be such. And I also believe that in this Gospel of the Witches we have a trustworthy outline at least of the doctrine and rites observed at these meetings. They adored forbidden deities and practised forbidden deeds, inspired as much by rebellion against Society as by their own passions.

There is, however, in the Evangel of the Witches an effort made to distinguish between the naturally wicked or corrupt and those who are outcasts or oppressed, as appears from the passage :—

"Yet like Cain's daughter (offspring) thou shalt never be,
Nor like the race who have become at last
Wicked and infamous from suffering,
As are the Jews and wandering Zingari,
Who are *all* thieves : like them ye shall *not* be."

The supper of the Witches, the cakes of meal, salt, and honey, in the form of crescent moons, are known to every classical scholar. The moon or horn-shaped cakes are still common. I have eaten of them this very day, and though they are known all over the world, I believe they owe their fashion to tradition.

In the conjuration of the meal there is a very curious tradition introduced to the effect that the *spige* or glittering grains of wheat from which spikes shoot like sun-rays, owe their brilliant likeness to a resemblance to the fire-fly, "who comes to give them light." We have, I doubt not, in this a classic tradition, but I cannot verify it. Hereupon the *Vangelo* cites a common nursery-rhyme, which may also be found in a nursery-tale, yet which, like others, is derived from witch-lore, by which the *lucciola* is put under a glass and conjured to give by its light certain answers.

The conjuration of the meal or bread, as being literally our body as contributing to form it, and deeply sacred because it had lain in the earth, where dark and wondrous secrets bide, seems to cast a new light on the Christian sacrament. It is a type of resurrection from the earth, and was therefore used at the Mysteries and Holy Supper, and the grain had pertained to *chthonic* secrets, or to what had been under the earth in darkness. Thus even earth-worms are invoked in modern witchcraft as familiar with dark mysteries, and the shepherd's pipe to win the Orphic power must be buried three days in the earth. And so all was, and is, in sorcery a kind of wild poetry based on symbols, all blending into one another, light and darkness, fire-flies and grain, life and death.

Very strange indeed, but very strictly according to ancient magic as described by classic authorities, is the threatening *Diana*, in case she will not grant a prayer. This recurs continually in the witch-exorcisms or spells. The *magus*, or witch, worships the spirit, but claims to have the right, drawn from a higher power, to *compel* even the Queen of Earth, Heaven, and Hell to grant the request. "Give me what I ask, and thou shalt have honour and offerings; refuse, and I will vex thee by insult." So Canidia and her kind boasted that they could *compel* the gods to appear. This is all classic. No one ever heard of a Satanic witch invoking or threatening the Trinity, or Christ or even the angels or saints. In fact, they cannot even *compel* the devil or his imps to obey—they work entirely by his good-will as slaves. But in the old Italian lore the sorcerer or witch is all or nothing, and aims at limitless will or power.

Of the ancient belief in the virtues of a perforated stone I need not speak. But it is to be remarked that in the invocation the witch goes forth *in the earliest morning* to seek for verbena or vervain. The ancient Persian magi, or rather their daughters, worshipped the sun as it rose by waving freshly plucked verbena,[1] which was one of the seven most powerful plants in magic. These Persian priestesses were naked while they thus worshipped, nudity being a symbol of truth and sincerity.

The extinguishing the lights, nakedness, and the orgie, were regarded as symbolical of the body being laid in the ground, the grain being planted, or of entering into darkness and death, to be revived in new forms, or regeneration and light. It was the laying aside of daily life.

The Gospel of the Witches, as I have given it, is in reality only the initial chapter of the collection of ceremonies, "cantrips," incantations, and traditions current in the fraternity or sisterhood, the whole of which are in the main to be found in my *Etruscan Roman Remains* and *Florentine Legends*. I have, it is true, a great number as yet unpublished, and there are more ungathered, but the whole scripture of this sorcery, all its principal tenets, formulas, medicaments, and mysteries may be found in what I have collected and printed. Yet I would urge that it would be worth while to arrange and edit it all into one work, because it would be to every student of archæology, folk-lore, or history of great value. It has been the faith of millions in the past; it has made itself felt in innumerable traditions, which deserve to be better understood than they are, and I would gladly undertake the

[1] FRIEDRICH, *Symbolik*, p. 283.

work if I believed that the public would make it worth the publisher's outlay and pains.

It may be observed with truth that I have not treated this Gospel, nor even the subject of witchcraft, entirely as *folk-lore*, as the word is strictly defined and carried out; that is, as a mere traditional fact or thing to be chiefly regarded as a variant like or unlike sundry other traditions, or to be tabulated and put away in pigeon-holes for reference. That it is useful and sensible to do all this is perfectly true, and it has led to an immense amount of valuable search, collection, and preservation. But there is this to be said—and I have observed that here and there a few genial minds are beginning to awake to it—that the mere study of the letter in this way has developed a great indifference to the spirit, going in many cases so far as to produce, like Realism in Art (to which it is allied), even a contempt for the matter or meaning of it, as originally believed in.

I was lately much struck by the fact that in a very learned work on Music, the author, in discussing that of ancient times and of the East, while extremely accurate and minute in determining pentatonic and all other scales, and what may be called the mere machinery and history of composition, showed that he was utterly ignorant of the fundamental fact that notes and chords, bars and melodies, were in themselves *ideas* or thoughts. Thus *Confucius* is said to have composed a melody which was a personal description of himself. Now if this be not understood, we cannot understand the soul of early music, and the folk-lorist who cannot get beyond the letter and fancies himself "scientific" is exactly like the musician who has no idea of how or why melodies were anciently composed.

The strange and mystical chapter "How Diana made the Stars and the Rain" is the same given in my *Legends of Florence*, vol. ii. p. 229, but much enlarged, or developed to a cosmogonic-mythologic sketch. And here a reflection occurs which is perhaps the most remarkable which all this Witch Evangel suggests. In all other Scriptures of all races, it is the male, Jehovah, Buddha, or Brahma, who creates the universe; in Witch Sorcery it is the female who is the primitive principle. Whenever in history there is a period of radical intellectual rebellion against long-established conservatism, hierarchy, and the like, there is always an effort to regard Woman as the fully equal, which means the superior sex. Thus in the extraordinary war of conflicting elements, strange schools of sorcery, Neo-Platonism, Cabala, Heretic Christianity, Gnosticism, Persian Magism and Dualism, with the remains of old Greek and Egyptian theologies in the third and fourth centuries at Alexandria, and in the House of Light of Cairo in the ninth, the equality of Woman was a prominent doctrine. It was Sophia or Helena, the enfranchised, who was then the true Christ who was to save mankind.

When Illumination or Illuminé-ism, in company with magic and mysticism, and a resolve to regenerate society according to extreme free-thought, inspired the Templars to the hope that they would master the Church and the world, the equality of Woman, derived from the Cairene traditions, again received attention. And it may be observed that during the Middle Ages, and even so late as the intense excitements which inspired the French Huguenots, the Jansenists and the Anabaptists, Woman always came forth more prominently or played a far greater part than she had done in social or political life. This was also the case in the Spiritualism founded by the Fox sisters of Rochester, New York, and it is manifesting itself in many ways in the *Fin de Siècle*, which is also a nervous chaos according to *Nordau*, — Woman being evidently a fish who shows herself most when the waters are troubled :—

> "Oh, Woman, in our hours of ease!"

The reader will remember the rest. But we should also remember that in the earlier ages the vast majority of mankind itself, suppressed by the too great or greatly abused power of Church and State, only manifested itself at such periods of rebellion against forms or ideas grown old. And with every new rebellion, every fresh outburst or *debâcle* or wild inundation and bursting over the barriers, humanity and woman gain something, that is to say, their just dues or rights. For as every freshet spreads more widely its waters over the fields, which are in due time the more fertilised thereby, so the world at large gains by every Revolution, however terrible or repugnant it may be for a time.

The Emancipated or Woman's Rights woman, when too enthusiastic, generally considers man as limited, while Woman is destined to gain on him. In earlier ages a contrary opinion prevailed, and both are, or were, apparently in the wrong, so far as the future is concerned. For in truth both sexes are progressive, and progress in this respect means not a *conflict* of the male and female principle, such as formed the basis of the *Mahabarata*, but a gradual ascertaining of true ability and adjustment of relations or co-ordination of powers—in doing which on a scientific basis all conflict ceases.

These remarks are appropriate to my text and subject, because it is in studying the epochs when woman has made herself prominent and influential that we learn what the capacities of the female sex truly are. Among these, that of Witchcraft as it truly was—not as it is generally quite misunderstood—is as deeply interesting as any other. For the *Witch*—laying aside all question as to magic or its non-existence—was once a real factor or great power in rebellious social life, and to this very day—as most novels bear witness—it is recognised that there is something uncanny, mysterious, and incomprehensible in woman, which neither she herself nor man can explain.

"For every woman is at heart a witch."

We have banished the broom and the cat and the working miracles, the Sabbat and pacts with Satan, but the mystery or puzzle is as great as ever; no one living knows to what it is destined to lead. Are not the charms of love of every kind, and the enjoyment of beauty in all its forms in nature, mysteries, miracles, or magical?

To all who are interested in this subject of woman's influence and capacity, this Evangel of the Witches will be of value as showing that there have been strange thinkers who regarded creation as a feminine development or parthenogenesis from which the masculine principle was born. Lucifer, or Light, lay hidden in the darkness of *Diana*, as heat is hidden in ice. But the regenerator or Messiah of this strange doctrine is a woman—ARADIA, though the two, mother and daughter, are confused or reflected in the different tales, even as *Jahveh* is confused with the *Elohim*.

"Remains to be said"—that the Adam-nable and Eve-il, or Adamite assemblages enjoined in the Gospel of Sorcery, are not much, if at all, kept up by the now few and far between old or young witches and venerable wizards of the present day. That is to say, not to my knowledge in Central or Northern Italy. But among the *roués*, *viveurs*, and fast women of Florence and Milan—where they are not quite as rare as eclipses—such assemblies are called *balli angelici* or angels' balls. They are indeed far from being unknown in any of the great cities of the world. A few years ago a Sunday newspaper in an American city published a detailed account of them in the "dance-houses" of the town, declaring that they were of very frequent occurrence, which was further verified to me by men familiar with them.

A very important point to all who regard the finds or discoveries of ancient tradition as of importance, is that a deep and extensive study of the Italian witch-traditions which I have collected, a comparison of them one with the other, and of the whole with what resembles it in the writings of Ovid and other mythologists, force the conviction (which I have often expressed, but not too frequently) that there are in these later records many very valuable and curious remains of ancient Latin or Etruscan lore, in all probability entire poems, tales, and invocations which have passed over from the ancient tongue. If this be *true*, and when it shall come to pass that scholars will read with interest what is here given, then most assuredly there will be critical examination and verification of what is ancient in it, and it will be discovered what marvels of tradition still endure.

That the witches even yet form a fragmentary secret society or sect, that they call it that of the Old Religion, and that there are in the Romagna entire villages in which the people are completely heathen, and almost entirely governed by *Settimani* or "seven months' children," may be read in the novel of that name, as well as several papers published in divers magazines, or accepted from my own personal knowledge. The existence of a *religion* supposes a Scripture, and in this case it may be admitted, almost without severe verification, that the Evangel of the Witches is really a very old work. Thus it is often evident that where a tradition has been taken down from verbal delivery, the old woman repeats words or sentences by whole chapters which she does not fully understand, but has heard and learned. These are to be verified by correlation or comparison with other tales and texts. Now considering all this most carefully and critically, or severely yet impartially, no one can resist the conviction that in this Gospel of the Witches we have a book which is in all probability the translation of some early or later Latin work, since it seems most probable that every fixed faith finds its record. There are literary men among the Pariahs of India; there were probably many among the minions of the moon, or nocturnal worshippers of *Diana*. In fact, I am not without hope that research may yet reveal in the writings of some long-forgotten heretic or mystic of the dark ages the parallel of many passages in this text, if not the whole of it.

Yet a few years, reader, and all this will have vanished from among the Italians before the newspaper and railroad, even as a light cloud is driven before a gale, or pass away like snow-flakes in a pond. Old traditions are, in fact, disappearing with such incredible rapidity that I am assured on best authority—and can indeed see for myself—that what I collected or had recorded for me ten years ago in the Romagna Toscana, with exceptionably skilful aid, could not now be gathered at all by anybody, since it no longer exists, save in the memories of a few old sorcerers who are daily disappearing, leaving no trace behind. It is going—going—it is all but gone; in fact, I often think that, old as I am (and I am twelve years beyond the limit of extreme old age as defined by the Duke of Marlborough in his defence), I shall yet live to hear the rap of the auctioneer Time as he bids off the last real Latin sorcerer to Death! It may be that he is passing in his checks even as I write. The women or witches, having more vitality, will last a little longer—I mean the traditional kind; for as regards innate natural dev-elopment of witchcraft and pure cus-tom, we shall always have with us sorceresses, even as we shall have the poor—until we all go up together.

What is very remarkable, even to the being difficult to understand, is the fact that so much antique tradition survived with so little change among the peasantry. But legends and spells in families of hereditary witches are far more likely to live than fashions in art, yet even the latter have been kept since 2000 years. Thus, as E. Neville Rolfe writes: "The late Signor Castellani, who was the first to reproduce with fidelity the jewellery found in the tombs of Etruria and Greece, made up his mind that some survival of this ancient and exquisite trade must still exist somewhere in Italy. He accordingly made diligent search . . . and in an out of the way village discovered goldsmiths who made ornaments for the peasants, which in their character indicated a strong survival of early Etruscan art."[1]

[1] I am here reminded, by a strange coincidence, that I having rediscovered the very ancient and lost art of the Chinese how to make bottles or vases on which inscriptions, &c., appeared when wine was poured into them, communicated the discovery on the spot where I made it to the brother of Signor Castellani; Sir Austin Layard, who had sent for him to hear and judge of it, being present. Signor Castellani the younger was overseer of the glass-works at Murano, in which I made the discovery. Signor Castellani said that he had read of these Chinese vases, and always regarded the story as a fable or impossible, but that they could be made perfectly by my process, adding, however, that they would cost too much to make it profitable. I admit that I have little faith in lost arts beyond recovering. Described in my book (unpublished) on the *Hundred Minor Arts*.

And here I would remark, that where I have written perhaps a little too bitterly of the indifference of scholars to the curious traditions preserved by wizards and witches, I refer to Rome, and especially to Northern Italy. *G. Pitré* did all that was possible for one man as regards the South. Since the foregoing chapters were written, I received *Naples in the Nineties*, by E. Neville Rolfe, B.A., in which a deep and intelligent interest in the subject is well supported by extensive knowledge. What will be to the reader of my book particularly interesting is the amount of information which Mr. Rolfe gives regarding the connection of *Diana* with witchcraft, and how many of her attributes became those of the Madonna. "The worship of Diana," as he says, "prevailed very extensively . . . so much so, that when Christianity superseded Paganism, much of the heathen symbolism was adapted to the new rites, and the transition from the worship of Diana to that of the Madonna was made comparatively simple." Mr. Rolfe speaks of the key, rue, and verbena as symbols of Diana; of all of these I have incantations, apparently very ancient, and identified with Diana. I have often found *rue* in houses in Florence, and had it given to me as a special favour. It is always concealed in some dark corner, because to take any away is to take luck. The bronze frog was an emblem of Diana; hence the Latin proverb, "He who loves a frog regards it as Diana." It was made till recent times as an amulet. I have one as a paper-weight now before me. There is also an incantation to the frog.

That wherein Mr. Rolfe tacitly and unconsciously confirms what I have written, and what is most remarkable in this my own work, is that the wizards in Italy form a distinct class, still exercising great power in Naples and Sicily, and even possessing very curious magical documents and cabalistic charts, one of which (familiar to those who have seen it among the *Takruri* and Arab sorcerers in Cairo, in their books) he gives. These probably are derived from Malta. Therefore it will not seem astonishing to the reader that this Gospel of the Witches should have been preserved, even as I have given it. That I have not had or seen it in an *old* MS. is certainly true, but that it has been written of yore, and is still repeated here and there orally, in separate parts, I am sure.[1]

It would be a great gratification to me if any among those into whose hands this book may fall, who may possess information confirming what is here set forth, would kindly either communicate it or publish it in some form, so that it may not be lost.

[1] In a very recent work by Messrs. Niceforo and Sighele, entitled *La Mala Vita a Roma* ("Evil Life in Rome"), there is a chapter devoted to the Witches of the Eternal City, of whom the writer says they form a class so hidden that "the most Roman of Romans is perhaps ignorant of their existence." This is true of the real *Strega*, though not of mere fortune-tellers, who are common enough.

THE CHILDREN OF DIANA, OR HOW THE FAIRIES WERE BORN

ALL things were made by Diana, the great spirits of the stars, men in their time and place, the giants which were of old, and the dwarfs who dwell in the rocks, and once a month worship her with cakes.

There was once a young man who was poor, without parents, yet was he good.

One night he sat in a lonely place, yet it was very beautiful, and there he saw a thousand little fairies, shining white, dancing in the light of the full moon.

"Gladly would I be like you, O fairies!" said the youth, "free from care, needing no food. But what are ye?"

"We are moon-rays, the children of Diana," replied one:—

"We are children of the Moon,
We are born of shining light;
When the Moon shoots forth a ray,
Then it takes a fairy's form.

"And thou art one of us because thou wert born when the Moon, our mother Diana, was full; yes, our brother, kin to us, belonging to our band.

"And if thou art hungry and poor . . . and wilt

have money in thy pocket, then think upon the Moon, on Diana, unto whom thou wert born; then repeat these words:—

"'Luna mia, bella Luna!
Più di una altra stella;
Tu sei sempre bella!
Portatemi la buona fortuna!'

"'Moon, Moon, beautiful Moon!
Fairer far than any star;
Moon, O Moon, if it may be,
Bring good fortune unto me!'

"And then, if thou hast money in thy pocket, thou wilt have it doubled.

"For the children who are born in a full moon are sons or daughters of the Moon, especially when they are born of a Sunday when there is a high tide.

"'Alta marea, luna piena, sai,
Grande uomo sicuro tu sarei.'

"'Full moon, high sea,
Great man shalt thou be!'"

Then the young man, who had only a *paolo*[1] in his purse, touched it, saying:—

"Luna mia, bella Luna,
Mia sempre bella Luna!"

"Moon, Moon, beautiful Moon,
Ever be my lovely Moon!"

---

[1] Fivepence Roman money.

And so the young man, wishing to make money, bought and sold and made money, which he doubled every month.

But it came to pass that after a time, during one month he could sell nothing, so made nothing. So by night he said to the Moon—

"Luna mia, Luna bella!
Che io amo più di altra stella!
Dimmi perche e fatato
Che io gnente (niente) ho guadagnato?"

"Moon, O Moon, whom I by far
Love beyond another star,
Tell me why it was ordained
That I this month have nothing gained?"

Then there appeared to him a little shining elf, who said:—

"Tu non devi aspettare
Altro che l' aiutare,
Quando fai ben lavorare."

"Money will not come to thee,
Nor any help or aid can'st see,
Unless you work industriously."

Then he added:—

"Io non daro mai denaro
Ma l' aiuto, mio caro!"

"Money I ne'er give, 'tis clear,
Only help to thee, my dear!"

Then the youth understood that the Moon, like God and Fortune, does the most for those who do the most for themselves.

> "Come l' appetito viene mangiando,
> E viene il guadagno lavorando e risparmiando."

> "As appetite comes by eating and craving,
> Profit results from labour and saving."

To be born in a full moon means to have an enlightened mind, and a high tide signifies an exalted intellect and full of thought. It is not enough to have a fine boat of Fortune.

> "Bisogna anche lavorare
> Per farla bene andare."

> "You must also bravely row,
> If you wish the bark to go."

> "Ben faremmo e ben diremmo,
> Mal va la barca senza remo."

> "Do your best, or talk, but more
> To row the boat you'll need an oar."

And, as it is said—

> "La fortuna a chi dà
> A chi toglie cosi sta,
> Qualche volta agli oziosi
> Ma il più ai laboriosi."

> "Fortune gives and Fortune takes,
> And to man a fortune makes,
> Sometimes to those who labour shirk,
> But oftener to those who work."

DIANA, QUEEN OF THE SERPENTS, GIVER OF THE GIFT OF LANGUAGES

IN a long and strange legend of *Melambo*, a magian and great physician of divine birth, there is an invocation to Diana which has a proper place in this work. The incident in which it occurs is as follows:—

One day Melambo asked his mother how it was that while it had been promised that he should know the language of all living things, it had not yet come to pass.

And his mother replied:—

"Patience, my son, for it is by waiting and watching ourselves that we learn how to be taught. And thou hast within thee the teachers who can impart the most, if thou wilt seek to hear them; yes, the professors who can teach thee more in a few minutes than others learn in a life."

It befell that one evening Melambo, thinking on this while playing with a nest of young serpents which his servant had found in a hollow oak, said:—

"I would that I could talk with you;
Well I know that ye have a language,
As graceful as your movement,
As brilliant as your colour."

Then he fell asleep, and the young serpents twined in his hair and began to lick his lips and eyes, while their mother sang:—

"Diana! Diana! Diana!
Regina delle strege!
E della notte oscura,
E di tutta la natura!
Delle stelle e della luna,
E di tutta la fortuna!
Tu che reggi la marea,
Che risplendi il mare nella sera!
Colla luce sulle onde,
La padrona sei del oceano,
Colla tua barca, fatta,
Fatta à mezza luna,
La tua barca rilucente,
Barca e luna crescente;
Fai sempre velo in cielo,
E in terra sulla sera,
E anche à navigare
Riflettata sulla mare,
Preghiamo di dare a questo,
Questo buon Melambo,
Qualunque parlare
Di qualunque animali!"

The Invocation of the Serpents' Mother to Diana.

"Diana! Diana! Diana!
Queen of all enchantresses
And of the dark night,

And of all nature,
Of the stars and of the moon,
And of all fate or fortune!
Thou who rulest the tide,
Who shinest by night on the sea,
Casting light upon the waters;
Thou who art mistress of the ocean
In thy boat made like a crescent,
Crescent moon-bark brightly gleaming,
Ever smiling high in heaven,
Sailing too on earth, reflected
In the ocean, on its water;
We implore thee give this sleeper,
Give unto this good Melambo
The great gift of understanding
What all creatures say while talking!"

This legend contains much that is very curious; among other things an invocation to the fire-fly, one to Mefitia, the goddess of malaria, and a long poetic prophecy relative to the hero. It is evidently full of old Latin mythologic lore of a very marked character. The whole of it may be found in a forthcoming work by the writer of this book, entitled, "The Unpublished Legends of Virgil." London, Elliot Stock.

DIANA AS GIVING BEAUTY AND RESTORING STRENGTH

DIANA hath power to do all things, to give glory to the lowly, wealth to the poor, joy to the afflicted, beauty to the ugly. Be not in grief, if you are her follower; though you be in prison and in darkness, she will bring light: many there are whom she sinks that they may rise the higher.

There was of old in Monteroni a young man so ugly that when a stranger was passing through the town he was shown this Gianni, for such was his name, as one of the sights of the place. Yet, hideous as he was, because he was rich, though of no family, he had confidence, and hoped boldly to win and wed some beautiful young lady of rank.

Now there came to dwell in Monteroni a wonderfully beautiful *biondina*, or blonde young lady of culture and condition, to whom Gianni, with his usual impudence, boldly made love, getting, as was also usual, a round No for his reply.

But this time, being more than usually fascinated in good truth, for there were influences at work he knew not of, he became as one possessed or mad with passion, so that he hung about the lady's house by night and day, seeking indeed an opportunity to rush in and seize her, or by some desperate trick to master and bear her away.

But here his plans were defeated, because the lady had ever by her a great cat which seemed to be of more than human intelligence, and, whenever Gianni approached her or her home, it always espied him and gave the alarm with a terrible noise. And there was indeed something so unearthly in its appearance, and something so awful in its great green eyes which shone like torches, that the boldest man might have been appalled by them.

But one evening Gianni reflected that it was foolish to be afraid of a mere cat, which need only scare a boy, and so he boldly ventured on an attack. So going forth, he took a ladder, which he carried and placed against the lady's window. But while he stood at the foot, he found by him an old woman, who earnestly began to beg him not to persevere in his intention. "For thou knowest well, Gianni," she said, "that the lady will have none of thee; thou art a terror to her. Do but go home and look in the glass, and it will seem to thee that thou art looking on mortal sin in human form."

Then Gianni in a roaring rage cried, "I will have my way and my will, thou old wife of the devil, if I must kill thee and the girl too!" Saying which, he rushed up the ladder; but before he had opened or could enter the window, and was at the top, he found himself as it were turned to wood or stone, unable to move.

Then he was overwhelmed with shame, and said,

"Ere long the whole town will be here to witness my defeat. However, I will make one last appeal." So he cried:—

"Oh, *vecchia!* thou who didst mean me more kindly than I knew, pardon me, I beg thee, and rescue me from this trouble! And if, as I well ween, thou art a witch, and if I, by becoming a wizard, may be freed from my trials and troubles, then I pray thee teach me how it may be done, so that I may win the young lady, since I now see that she is of thy kind, and that I must be of it to be worthy of her."

Then Gianni saw the old woman sweep like a flash of light from a lantern up from the ground, and, touching him, bore him away from the ladder, when lo! the light was a cat, who had been anon the witch, and she said:—

"Thou wilt soon set forth on a long journey, and in thy way thou wilt find a wretched worn-out horse, when thou must say:—

"'Fata Diana! Fata Diana! Fata Diana!
Io vi scongiuro
Di dare un po di bene,
A quella povera bestia!'
E poi si trovera
Una grossa capra,
Ma un vero caprone,
E tu dirai:
'Bona sera, bel caprone,'
E questo ti risponderà
'Buona sera galantuomo

Sono tanto stanco, io
Che non mi sento—
Di andare più avanti.'
E risponderai al solito,
'Fata Diana, vi scongiuro,
Di dare pace e bene
A questo caprone!'

"'Fairy Diana! Fairy Diana! Fairy Diana!
I conjure thee to do some little good
To this poor beast.'
Then thou wilt find
A great goat,
A true he-goat,
And thou shalt say,
'Good evening, fair goat!
And he will reply,
'Good evening, fair sir!
I am so weary
That I can go no farther.'
And thou shalt reply as usual,
'Fairy Diana, I conjure thee
To give to this goat relief and peace!'

"Then will *we* enter in a great hall where thou wilt see many beautiful ladies who will try to fascinate thee; but let thy answer ever be, 'She whom I love is her of Monteroni.'

"And now, Gianni, to horse; mount and away!" So he mounted the cat, which flew as quick as thought, and found the mare, and having pronounced over it the incantation, it became a woman and said:—

"In nome della Fata Diana!
Tu possa divenire
Un giovane bello
Bianco e rosso!
Di latte e sangue!"

"In the name of the Fairy Diana!
Mayest thou hereby become
A beautiful young man,
Red and white in hue,
Like to milk and blood!"

After this he found the goat and conjured it in like manner, and it replied:—

"In the name of the Fairy Diana!
Be thou attired more richly than a prince!"

So he passed to the hall, where he was wooed by beautiful ladies, but his answer to them all was that his love was at Monterone.

Then he saw or knew no more, but on awaking found himself in Monterone, and so changed to a handsome youth that no one knew him. So he married his beautiful lady, and all lived the hidden life of witches and wizards from that day, and are now in Fairy Land.

NOTE

As a curious illustration of the fact that the faith in Diana and the other deities of the Roman mythology, as connected with divination, still survives among the Italians of "the people," I may mention that after this work went to press, I purchased for two soldi or one penny, a small chapbook in which it is shown how, by a process of conjuration or evocation and numbers, not only Diana, but thirty-nine other deities may be made to give answers to certain questions. The work is probably taken from some old manuscript, as it is declared to have been discovered and translated by P. P. Francesco di Villanova Monteleone. It is divided into two parts, one entitled *Circe* and the other *Medea.*

As such works must have pictures, Circe is set forth by a page cut of a very ugly old woman in the most modern costume of shawl and mob-cap with ribbons. She is holding an ordinary candlestick. It is quite the ideal of a common fortune-teller, and it is probable that the words *Maga Circe* suggested nothing more or less than such a person to him who "made up" the book. That of Medea is, however, quite correct, even artistic, representing the sorceress as conjuring the magic bath, and was probably taken from some work on mythology. It is ever so in Italy, where the most grotesque and modern conceptions of classic subjects are mingled with much that is accurate and beautiful—of which indeed this work supplies many examples.